CHANGE

ALSO BY ILCHI LEE

The Call of Sedona

Healing Society

The Twelve Enlightenments for Healing Society

Brain Wave Vibration

In Full Bloom

Principles of Brain Management

Healing Chakras

Earth Citizen

Mago's Dream

Human Technology

LifeParticle Meditation

CHANGE

REALIZING YOUR
GREATEST
POTENTIAL

ILCHI LEE

**BEST
LIFE**

BEST Life Media
6560 State Route 179, Suite 114
Sedona, AZ 86351
www.bestlifemedia.com
877-504-1106

First paperback edition: September 2013
Library of Congress Control Number: 2013941541
ISBN-13: 978-1-935127-58-1
Cover and interior design by Malou Leontsinis.

With thanks to my fellow Earth citizens
who strive to change for the benefit of all.

CONTENTS

INTRODUCTION

Recovering Our True Greatness

Everyone wants to be happy. Nature has programmed all of us with this powerful motivating force and endowed us with the energy and intelligence to work toward attaining fulfillment in our lives. Why?

Do you suppose this inherent desire for a happy life is there to make us miserable when we run into the inevitable obstacles, inside us or in the world, that block our progress and thwart our efforts to achieve our goals?

I don't think so. My experience tells me that Mother Nature, in her infinite kindness, has implanted this evolutionary urge deep in the mysteries of our consciousness and the spiral strands of our DNA to keep us *growing*, moving ever forward toward a fulfillment we can only dimly discern and define but that we *know* is our ultimate birthright—the place where we are born to dwell.

Sometimes the strong current of life carries us forward effortlessly from one success to another, from one level of achievement or one experience of love to a higher level, and we feel happy and that life is good. Sometimes as we float on the current we crash into a boulder—failure, rejection, or simply the uncertainty of where we really want to go. At times like these—and we *all* have them, including me—we can blame the environment, the person or group that is blocking or rejecting us, the economy, the political party in power, our spouse, our parents . . . or we can take an honest look in the mirror and work on ways to change ourselves so that no matter how difficult the outward conditions of our life may appear to be, we can find the resources to overcome them, to change and thrive.

Are you in a place now where you want to see some changes in your life? Perhaps you want to get yourself on an exercise program and lose some weight, upgrade your job or career, or restore a broken relationship. Or maybe you're feeling some serious concern about the state and direction of the world, global warming, environmental devastation, terrorism, international crises and tensions that could so easily escalate or explode, and you want to do something to change it all.

The desire for change, in ourselves and our world, begins with dissatisfaction about the way things are—a sense that something is wrong or could be better—that the life I am now living is not the life I was meant to live. Maybe what we want is not so much to change, but to realize who we are deep inside, to grow into our true selves, to know ourselves more deeply. Maybe we want to fill a void we sense in our life, as if something real is missing or as if there is a hole in our soul.

That is how my own seeking started. When I was young, I felt like a misfit in a world that everyone else seemed to think was just fine. I was desperate because living year after year with the sense of being a misfit was unbearable to me, as it would be to anyone. I felt that something was not right, either with me or the rest of the world—or both. Because the world was too big for me to comprehend, inevitably my choice was to look into myself.

I was plagued with countless *Me* questions, such as: Why am I here? Why am I not happy? Why am I not functioning well, and why am I not fitting in, as others do? Why does the world look strange to me while it seems to look all right to others? Why don't other people ask questions like the ones I'm always asking?

I would go around and around on these questions, never coming up with satisfactory answers; and then, no matter where I started, I always ended up asking the same one basic question: *Who am I really?* Every time, the question became deeper as my desire to know grew stronger until it became my single unwavering focus, whether I was awake or asleep.

The answer finally came. In a glorious moment on a mountaintop in Korea, after a rigorous solo retreat that included long hours of meditation, martial arts practice, breathing exercises, and fasting—I awakened to the truth of who I am. I saw that I was not the small, limited self I had thought myself to be. I was not my body or my personality. The real I was universal: my mind was cosmic mind; my energy was cosmic, universal energy. That was the bottom line, the truth of who I am.

With that answer, everything else that I needed to know about life fell into place.

And I discovered something extremely valuable and important: it's only when we get deep down to the very basis of reality, the silent foundation of life, that we attain the power and wisdom to create the changes we desire, not only in our individual life but also in the world. By becoming awakened to what is boundless and unchanging, I found that changes became more natural and easier to produce. Realizing that I was timeless and changeless gave me a place to stand and a kind of leverage.

It is like taking off tinted glasses you've been wearing for so long that you've forgotten you were wearing them. With realization of your true self, you become able to see clearly, and to choose which glasses you want to wear and the colors you want to see, while maintaining awareness of the changeless pure light shining through the diverse colors. You become able to create meaning and value in life. The once-gray world starts shining with vibrant energy, and your life is filled with meaning, purpose, and joy.

That awakening occurred about 33 years ago. Since then, my life's work has been to share what I realized with the world. My experience itself didn't change. But I have constantly reflected upon my own experiences to see more fully what I have to offer, and I have revised and reinvented the ways that I communicate my experiences and thoughts with other people. This book is the most recent update.

I am culturally indebted to the age-old Korean tradition

of Taoism. My studies of this great legacy of knowledge have shown me that my experiences are profoundly aligned with the teachings of this tradition. Sharing these teachings in the light of my experience of realization and awakening is one of the goals of this book.

Every page of the book will reflect my lifelong passion to find ever-better ways to develop our full human potential. I believe that we as a species have not realized the most precious qualities with which nature has endowed us, the abilities that will enable us to create lasting positive changes in our world. I believe that we will find the key to this development in our brain. Thus, much of my work in recent years has been about the brain. The past decade of scientific research has brought a treasury of knowledge about how the brain works and how its workings affect our health, happiness, and creativity and contribute to our spiritual awakening. I will share some of this knowledge with you in these pages.

In recent years, my interest has been especially focused on multimedia and the Internet. I believed by combining multiple sensory channels such as light, sound, and vibration, the brain could be stimulated more globally—and the message I wanted to share could be delivered more effectively. I also thought that experiencing an awakening to a new aspect of reality without the atmosphere of seriousness of so-called spiritual practices would make the essence of those spiritual practices more accessible to many people.

For example, wouldn't it be great if people became able to realize their true potential while watching a movie, even just for fun and interest? Needless to say, the accessibility of the Internet has made it the most powerful tool for sharing information and connecting to other people. The Internet has long been an integral part of my life, as it is to many others. Therefore, I dearly wished to make the stories I wanted to tell into a multimedia format and make the best use of the Internet by sharing them there.

Finally, in May 2013, my wishes resulted in the release of the movie *Change: The LifeParticle Effect*. I am glad many of the people I have been able to reach out to with this new medium have responded with enthusiasm. Also, I am working on a website, www.changeyourenergy.com, that provides more detailed support and guidance to those who have become interested in sharing the message of the movie and creating the changes that are presented through the stories.

The ultimate goal for everything I do, including creating movies and websites, is to help us explore and find ways to continue to grow as humanity in a balanced, peaceful, and sustainable manner. My privilege and joy is to work with my fellow Earth citizens toward this goal.

❧

If you sometimes find yourself wondering whether you are living the most meaningful life possible, or if you're confused because you feel your life could be better but don't know exactly what to change or where to start, this book will be helpful. In these pages, I will urge you to keep going deeper, sincerely asking yourself who you really are and what you really want.

Maybe you've already asked these questions many times.

However, if you feel there's still something missing in your life, or if you still see a gap, large or small, between the answers you have received and the life you actually live, I believe you need to keep asking.

I don't have any assumption about the answers you will discover on your journey, nor do I have any intention to suggest a specific direction for your seeking. However, by sharing my own experiences, I do hope to excite you about what is possible. In the course of my inner explorations, especially after my awakening, I discovered that I had a beautiful mind, a mind that desired to benefit all life-forms and all beings. I was deeply touched by the discovery of this goodness. Please don't misunderstand—it is not my achievement or creation. This universal goodness is something that has existed from primordial time. This greatness is a gift, a gift of deepest mystery.

Even more touching was the discovery that the same beautiful mind resides in everyone. This has given me great hope.

I have come to believe that the true power to create the changes we desire in our personal lives and in the world comes from this greatness within us. The rest of this book is for finding out what this greatness is and how we can use it.

Our world desperately needs change. We all know this. The scope of the change ranges from our lifestyles to the direction of our civilization. When we acknowledge our greatness and start living it, when we open our hearts to the natural kindness and the caring for all beings that resides within us, all these necessary transformations can begin.

CHAPTER ONE

We Need to Change

THE END OF THE WORLD

How was your winter solstice, December 21, 2012? Was there anything especially noticeable in your life on that day? Probably this was one of the most widely known and talked about dates in human history. Because the Mayan people were known to have unusual expertise in calculating long periods of time, and were believed to have secret knowledge about the universe, when it became well known that their calendar ended with December 21, 2012, many people interpreted it as a prophecy that the world would end on that day. Weight was added to the "end of the world" hypothesis because of its apparent agreement with other prophecies. As you will no doubt recall, this became a popular subject for thought and discussion.

Of course, that the Mayan people did not mention another year following 2012 did not necessarily mean they believed the world would cease to exist. More likely, they wanted to explain a cyclic change, the end of one era and the start of another, perhaps a much greater one—so it might be a cause for celebration rather than fear. Or perhaps they simply didn't have enough space for further writing! "End of the world" was the most publicized of many possible ways to interpret the calendar, but certainly not the only way—nor, as it turns out, the most accurate or prophetic.

Some believed, some doubted, many were just curious, and most of us were indifferent. What was your position? Did the concept of the end of the world seem like total nonsense to you—after all, when you think about it, what was the chance that this planet and its trillions of inhabitants would somehow disappear overnight? Or were you worried and uneasy about it?

I had both responses, but for a particular, long-standing reason. Regardless of the Mayan calendar or any other prophecy, I always see two opposite possibilities for the future of humanity. One is bright, and the other is dark. I am nervous because I feel every day we are losing a day's chance to strengthen the bright side, and thus getting closer to the point of no return.

A week before December 21, 2012, there was a tragedy that broke the hearts of billions of people not only in the United States but all over the world. I was in Korea at that time, but the shocking news traveled over the Pacific Ocean very quickly. I was stricken, just like you, by the news that 28 people, including 20 first-grade children, were killed in a school shooting in a small quiet town in Connecticut. Like many others, I was shocked speechless, with deep pain and sorrow. But at the same time, I felt a strong voice of determination arising from the unfathomable depth of sorrow. Something inside me shouted, "This must end!"

Watching clips from President Obama's press conference, I heard the same voice as if it were echoing in every heart broken by the pain and sorrow and in every mind that realized we all are responsible for what's happening now in our world. "We can't tolerate this anymore," the president said. "These tragedies must end. And to end them, we must change."

CAN WE AFFORD TO CONTINUE?

We have tried to change innumerable times, personally and collectively. The beginning of a new year is always an opportunity to make resolutions to become a better person and live a better life. Presidential elections are also chances for making pledges and forming expectations to build a better government and a better-off country. However, our efforts are not always successful, and in more cases than we'd like to admit, our resolutions, promises, and expectations don't bring the longed-for results. Even when we manage to make some changes, they often don't last or accomplish what we want to achieve, and we revert to our old patterns.

Some changes we feel we can control and put into effect on our own. But if we examine more carefully, we find that many of the things we want to change are inseparably wired into the life we share with other people in the local, national, and global communities. For example, the healthy lifestyle that you are determined to live, that you take to be a personal choice over which you have control, is heavily influenced and limited by the culture and industries of the community you belong to.

One aspect of your desire for a healthier life probably relates to diet. You'd like to eat fresh, natural food and a more balanced diet. But what if the cafeteria in the building where you work every day stocks and serves only fast foods? How easy would it be to adhere to the dietary principles you believe in? How far afield would you go, how much extra money would you be willing and able to spend on healthier food choices? It can be quite a challenge.

If you are like me, you want to prepare your meals with naturally grown ingredients. But if more than 90 percent of crops available in the market contain GMOs (genetically modified organisms), your options are very limited. This makes some changes difficult or almost impossible to implement. The systemic force of the society that keeps us on our present track is much stronger and deeper than it looks.

Since the beginning of our current civilization, the human population and our activities on this planet have steadily increased. War and disease have occasionally dented the upward curve of population growth, but they were merely a pause before a greater leap. As the population has grown, the using-up of natural resources has correspondingly increased, and so has the impact on the planet of this vital resources depletion.

One pattern that is found across the spectrum of human activity is known as exponential growth, which means we are not just increasing our activities, but also increasing the rate of increase. This is the way it works: Suppose you have 100 dollars to spend, and you start by spending 10 dollars. Every day, you double the amount you spend. What will happen? This is a question that a third or fourth grader can answer without even a blink of an eye. She will say, "Guess what: you are broke." You use up 10 dollars on day one, 20 dollars on day two, 40 dollars on day three, and then: there is no day four, you don't have 80 dollars left to spend. We call it unsustainable.

The increase looks small at the beginning, but soon the curve rises straight up like a rocket. The world population, energy consumption, expense for health care and defense, use of chemicals in agriculture, amount of waste we dump into earth, air, and water, number of incidents of lifestyle-related disease such as diabetes, obesity and cancers, and national debts are just a few examples of destructive growth that is exponential or nearly so.

We could afford to maintain this pattern of exponential growth if we had limitless resources. But we don't.

It is like trying to only breathe in, without exhalation. We all know what will happen if you keep breathing in without breathing out. Eventually you will exhale, but if you don't, your lungs will burst. Continuous external growth, like continuous inhaling, is not sustainable. But because we have been inhaling for so long, consuming for so long, even though we see that it can't go on this way, we don't know how to alter the pattern.

We have to recover our natural sense of balance, and slowly make a shift from inhaling to exhaling. Only when we exhale can we inhale again, and that's how life continues.

To see the truth as truth, we don't need a lot of study. It's not complicated. What we need is pure observation. An open mind and fresh eyes will serve us well.

Nothing particularly apocalyptic happened on December 21, 2012. This doesn't mean that humanity has passed a cosmic test and that we can continue on with our current pattern without having to face the cumulative consequences of our behavior. External growth, materialism, possession, competition and dominance have been key words in the paradigm driving human civilization. Within this paradigm, growth means more accumulation; development means greater capacity to produce things and thereby eventually turn natural resources into waste. Global and long-term outcomes of running such a destructive and wasteful civilization have not been considered.

The root of this mistaken paradigm is the faulty perception of ourselves as separate, isolated individuals, and the selfishness, greed, and competitiveness stemming from this perception. As long as this perspective predominates, and we continue to see the world through these glasses, nature will be viewed as wilderness to conquer and exploit, with other people and other life-forms seen as competitors to defeat and control if we are to survive and thrive.

Our technology and social institutions have advanced at a blinding rate, but because the mind that uses the technology and creates the institutions has remained unchanged, all these rapid developments have contributed to the increase of separation, conflicts, and devastation rather than decreasing them. The planetary ecosystem is being driven toward the point of no recovery. The global economy reveals a terrible imbalance of wealth in which more than a quarter of the world's population is surviving—and just barely surviving—on less than one dollar a day and 25,000 people, including 15,000 children, are dying of hunger every day. On the other hand, millions of people are overweight, and a tiny fraction of the population owns the vast majority of wealth.

These snapshots of the balance sheet of human civilization force us to ask: Is this really our best? Are we resigned to following the fate of the dinosaurs, despite having so much brainpower and technological capacity available to make things better? Is it too big a task to change the direction of our civilization? Are we too late? And if we still have a chance, where should we start?

The change doesn't need to be apocalyptic, but it does need to happen. Otherwise, life in the world will end anyway, simply because we cannot sustain it.

CHANGE SHOULD BE DEEP AND THOROUGH

One of the ways to assess the impact of human activities on this planet is what is known as the "ecological footprint." In order to stand, I need land the size of my two feet; that's my footprint. In order to lie down, I need land the size of my body flat on the ground. Likewise, all human activities, even the least productive ones, require a certain amount of surface area of the Earth, such as forests to provide wood, fisheries to breed fish, farmland for agriculture, and vacant ground for residential and commercial buildings. (Actually, the forest is not only for timbering, but also for breathing, as it converts the CO_2 generated by respiration into O_2 through photosynthesis.) The size of the surface area required for maintaining these activities is called the ecological footprint.

Because each country is on a different level of economic development that supports different lifestyles, the size of the ecological footprint varies from country to country. The current collective ecological footprint needed to successfully maintain the entire human population of the world is calculated to be one and a half times larger than the size of the Earth. If all countries choose to emulate the economic development of the United States, and all people choose to adopt the high consumption lifestyles of this country, the size will explode to five times larger than the Earth.

Unfortunately, especially in the rapidly industrializing large-population countries such as India and China, the world is blindly following this pattern in spite of the predictable dismal end. If we are not willing to scale back our lifestyle, we will need to create four more planet Earths in addition to the existing one. Can we?

This means that we cannot make a real difference in our global situation just by eating some more organic vegetables, driving a hybrid car, or practicing recycling a little more diligently. I am not denying the positive impact of these actions on our personal lives and on our planet. But if the values such as success, profit, and dominance that currently drive our lives personally and collectively remain the same, the impact of making these changes in our personal practices will be nominal.

Honestly, would you be willing to relinquish some of the comforts and benefits that you enjoy now, if you were convinced that there is truly a conflict between these personal goodies and the good of all?

Someone asked me how we can truly know what our values are. I said, "If you take a look at your checkbook and bank account, you will see what you care about and value most." We pay for what we really want. Do we really want peace? Do we really want sustainability?

How important does the Earth feel to me? If something is genuinely important to us, we will make it a priority, and this consideration will be reflected in the choices we make, especially in allocating our time and money. That's what the checkbook and the bank account records tell us. The same will apply to organizations, governments, and nations as well.

If we don't see real changes in the world, it simply means we are not serious enough about creating those changes. We cannot afford to entertain superficial changes any more. The changes we need should be deep, real, and thorough.

When the changes are deep, real, and thorough, they will affect our beliefs, perceptions, and experiences. We will see the world differently and experience our reality differently. Because we are so accustomed to our current ways of perceiving and evaluating our world, we may not be able to conceive any other possibilities. But after the changes have occurred, we may be surprised and wonder how we could have lived for such a long time within the limited and limiting boundaries of those perceptions, beliefs, and experiences.

IT IS TIME TO SLOW DOWN AND BREATHE OUT

Lately, I have been trying to imagine what the world will be like 10 years from now. Will we still have the luxury of dreaming about 10 years down the road, when we are 10 years down the road from today? We have traveled this road since the dawn of our current civilization. We walked at the beginning, and soon started to run. Over time, the runners have changed but not the direction in which they ran and are still running.

Then the pace of industry, technology, and civilization in general sped up, and we found ourselves on a moving train. We're still on that train, not because we're absolutely sure this is the right track to be on, but because there seems to be no other way. And we're beginning to feel a bit nervous. Could it be—as it seems more and more—that the train we're on doesn't have a driver? The scenery from the train windows is getting bleaker and bleaker, and the speed seems to be picking up. It's dawning on more of us every day that we might be on course to crash into the side of a mountain or fall off a cliff.

Because we're moving so fast, we can't suddenly stop. Nor can we change direction or go backward, simply to repeat the same mistake of traveling a road without knowing where we are heading. We have to slow down, take a deep breath of fresh air, and breathe out all the tension from our chest. We need—individually and collectively—to pause for reflection on where we are, where we want to go, and where we are actually heading. A long time ago, Lao Tzu, another person who was seriously interested in the Truth of life, said, "If you do not change direction, you may end up where you are heading." I agree. We need to reevaluate our priorities, set new goals, make a plan, and take action.

FROM THE EYE OF EGO TO THE EYE OF TAO

I would like to jump-start this process of reflection by asking one question: Is your brain positive or negative? If you are about to say both, let me ask the question differently: What's the default mode?

While you are reading this, if you hear a loud thud outside your house and don't know what it is, what will be the first thought that comes to mind? Will it be positive or negative? It might be the sound of a huge bag of money falling from the sky, but you would never think that way, would you? Instead, most likely you will say, "What's wrong?"

This is the brain's default mode. In psychology, it's known as "negatively biased." It's a mode of vigilance, a kind of negative anticipation in which we are on the alert for what's wrong or could be wrong. This is not as bad as it sounds, because this built-in response is useful for a very practical reason: the good things that happen to your life won't kill you. In fact, the more good things that come your way, the better. But a bad thing, even just one, can kill you. It could be an encounter with a tiger, a snake, or a bolt of lightning. It could be an armed robber, or a drone attack. Just one such incident could threaten your survival. We learned this throughout the history of our evolution, and we developed this negatively biased vigilance mode in our brain to protect ourselves—which has worked for millions of years.

Because of this default mode, we tend to designate anything new and unidentified as a potential threat. Automatically, we separate our territory from the threat and do our best to control the situation and protect our turf. Threat, separation, and the attempt to control are the key features of the world seen through the eyes of a separate individual self, the "ego," an imaginary, isolated, self-contained entity that all of us believe in until we see through it to the Source.

This mode of reacting stands out starkly when you are stressed, especially when you perceive something or someone as a threat to your security. In that situation, the most vital perception for you is the distinction between you (or your territory) and the "other." It can be your idea, your body, your money, your family, or whatever you feel to be yours—an extension of yourself—in that situation. You become sharply aware of your presence and your boundaries. Once your brain is in stress response gear, your focus is on how to survive, to win, or to defeat the "opponent." You will use all means available to achieve that goal, and being in control is crucial.

Because we developed this mode while we were still striving as a species toward the dominant position in competition with other species, its influence on our life goes much deeper, beyond personal behavioral patterns. This mode formed the foundation of the way we have been relating to the world in general, and goes something like this: We are all separate beings, and others (the rest of the world) are potential threats. Therefore we have to be stronger than others to beat them. In this model, Nature is not seen as a benevolent Mother, the source and support of life, but rather as wilderness, which is dangerous and needs to be conquered and civilized.

Even though we have refined our behavior over many centuries, the basic perception that we are individual beings, separate from the rest of the world, remains unchanged. Reflecting this age-old perception, the way we relate to the world remains unchanged, too.

The view of the world seen through the eye of Ego is very convincing and has been dominant for the greater part of human history. However, witnessing what's happening now in the world, we may well wonder—indeed we *must* ask—whether this view is correct and valid. Is it a skillful mode of perception, a useful approach to life?

Historically, this is not the only way we human beings have experienced our world. Over the millennia, numerous civilizations and their thought-leaders have viewed the world not as a battlefield or a hostile mixture of separate, potentially warring factions, but as a unified whole that includes the mind or consciousness that sees the world as such. Seeing the world as a whole means that you feel a connection with all of existence, and you don't grant a special position or give special meaning to your individual self in the big picture of the world and in the great circle of life.

Please join me for a moment to explore this perspective. Why should you do so? Because if you can assume this perspective, even just for a short while, the world will look quite different.

Let's think about *threat* first. When the weather turns cold, it can seem threatening if you are not ready, but the weather is not being mean to you personally—it doesn't intend to cause harm. The weather is simply doing what it does and has always done—changing with the seasons.

In the Arizona desert where I like to hike, the weather change is dramatic, as if there were only two seasons: summer and winter. Both come very quickly. When the weather gets cold suddenly, the change is detrimental to many wild flowers. If the seasons were to delay their cyclic transition just because they are "personally" concerned about the blossom of a wildflower that is not ready for the cold weather and is too young, beautiful, and unappreciated to die in frost, what would this mean? If Nature proceeded so personally, what would happen? There would be chaos. Nature, in part and as a whole, operates in accord with universal laws. There are no favorites, no exceptions or exemptions to the laws of nature. So what looks like a threat or a personal attack to the eye of Ego is actually a normal, natural occurrence when seen from the perspective of the whole.

Second, let's take a look at *separation*. I am drinking water now. If I see the water in the cup as separate from the other water resources of this planet, I am wrong. I will prove that this water is not separate from the rest of the water of the Earth in a couple of hours when I go to a bathroom to send the water out of my body back to the source. When seen through the perspective of the whole, separation is an illusion, too.

Third, what about *control*? Because separation is an illusion, control is also an illusion. Why? Because, how can a part control the whole that the part belongs to? I am looking at my little finger. I can lift my little finger, but the little finger cannot lift me. If a part persistently tries to control the whole, it will destroy the whole or more likely, the part will be removed before it destroys the whole. This will apply to us, the human species, in our relation to the Earth, too.

We need to change our way of seeing the world and relating to it, not because our current way is intrinsically bad or "evil," but because we have become too powerful to continue to live as we have been living. Whether we like it or not, collectively we have become the most powerful factor in determining not only the future of human society, but also the direction of the entire planet with all its life-forms. Already tens of thousands of species—colorful, vital, fascinating, important to themselves and to the balance and harmony of their ecosystems—have been obliterated. If we choose to maintain our current way, it—that is, we—eventually will destroy our world and ourselves.

The change we need is from the eye (*I*) that sees the world as a collection of separate beings who are threats to each other to the eye (*I*) that sees the world as a network of beings inseparably connected in a living whole. I would call this the transition *from the eye of Ego to the eye of Tao.*

The world seen through the eye of Tao will be very different. What we experience as a threat through the eye of Ego is simply change in the Big Picture of the whole. All are connected and separation is an illusion. We cannot control the whole, but we can learn to live with it as it is and as it evolves. Change, connectivity, and learning to live well with others and with Nature and her ways will be the features of the world when seen through the eye of Tao.

IS CHANGE POSSIBLE?

Change is the very nature of Nature. If there's one thing that doesn't change, it is the fact that everything changes. In the Korean tradition of Tao, this is called *impermanence*.

The teaching about impermanence can be summarized like this:

Anything that has a beginning must have an end. Anything that is created will change. Impermanence is the very nature of things. Realizing that nothing is permanent is the true beginning of enlightenment. Suffering comes from attachment that wants to hold something permanently that is not permanent in its intrinsic nature. Awakening to the truth of impermanence frees you from attachment.

Life, which is sustained by our effort to persist, is destined to cease. This inherent paradox of life provides the ground for suffering as a basic human condition. Failure to realize impermanence makes life an experience of suffering. Impermanence—change, transformation, growth, and the eventual death of our selves and all we hold dear—is a common condition of being human.

When we understand and accept this truth, we can stop being judgmental and become truly compassionate, humble, and grateful. Only then can we recognize the value and meaning of any thing or any experience, whatever it may be, and do what we do with sincerity and gratitude. Impermanence, instead of diminishing the value of things, makes us deeply appreciate the significance and preciousness of our experience at the present moment. This brings bliss.

It is significant that the world discovered by modern science is very close to the view of the world seen through the eye of Tao. (One of the first books to explore and explain this correspondence was in fact called *The Tao of Physics*, written by Fritjof Capra, then a young physicist at the University of California.) According to modern physics, the world at its most refined level exists as empty space vibrating with waves of probabilities, which suggests limitless potential for change.

What is more surprising—indeed stunning and difficult to grasp—is that these probabilities turn into a physical reality *through observation by a conscious mind*, which means your mind creates reality, literally. Because big things are made of small things, this applies not only to the tiny marginal units of matter, but also to big things such as you and me, and supposedly to the entire universe, meaning everything. The world is not as solid as it looks.

The universe likes change. Everything that appears so solid and substantial is built on the shifting sands of ceaseless transformation on the quantum level. Ironically, that's the one, steady, constant factor about the universe that you can count on: the universe is always changing. This is a positive and hopeful fact! It means that all our effort to change is supported by the very nature of Life.

THE ILLUSION OF MY LIFE

Even if we accept impermanence as a general principle of the universe, there's one thing to which we don't want to apply this principle. Can you guess what that is? It is My Life! We desire this to be an exception to the law of impermanence. We want to live forever, as "us," with our friends and all the things we love, everything we think of as "me" and "mine." However, this is another illusion that we need to overcome if we are to make the shift from the eye of Ego to the eye of Tao. This idea of My Life—as a separate, inherently existing entity—has its roots so deep in our minds that most of us cannot break free of it, even until the last moments of our life.

Now consider this. Which one of these two statements feels true: "I own life" or "Life owns me"? Certainly "life" does not care about ownership. But we think and behave as if we "own" life, certainly our own life. Isn't this the bottom-line belief behind the notion of My Life?

But think about it. In what way is it *your* life? Did you create it? Do you remember how you were born? Was your birth the beginning of your life? Or when was its beginning? When did you start being you? Was it from birth, the egg and sperm, genes—or what? Did somebody come to you and ask for your permission or agreement to be born? None of these were true. You were just born. When you were born, life was just there, inside and outside.

And how about the end? Will life send somebody to get your permission or agreement before it leaves you? No, it will leave without a notice or even a mere hint, much less permission or agreement.

If something comes to you without your permission and leaves you without any notice, how can you say it is yours? You didn't create life. Life created you. *Life is expressing itself through you* as it does through countless diverse forms. Life is not something that you can possess or control. Everything that I experience and recognize to be me or mine, including my body, is a phenomenon of life.

Like me, like all of us, you are a phenomenon of life, an expression of life. All that you can own about life are your experiences, and really, you can own only a portion of your experiences, in the form of memory. Even these memories won't last. At the last moment what will remain with you will be a vague feeling about the totality of your life experiences.

You, as a phenomenon like all phenomena, have a beginning and an end. When life takes a visible form, we call it birth, and when it dissolves into invisible energy, we call it death. From the perspective of life itself, it is all just change; nothing is "born" or "dies." Life, while expressing itself in countlessly diverse forms, is a continuous flow without a beginning or an end.

If this is the case, between a phenomenon that lasts only between the two points called birth and death, and life itself that underlies and makes possible not only this particular phenomenon but also all phenomena everywhere and at all times, which one is truly you? In some sense, this question is really dumb: could you possibly have difficulty choosing between what is truly real and lasting, something that, as an ancient Taoist book says, is "vast and eternally great" and something that is a temporary phenomenon, a blip on the radar screen of time?

The answer to this question is not something that only those who have achieved enlightenment through a highly advanced spiritual practice can realize. The answer is obvious to pure observation that sees things the way they are without attachment or denial. This simple observation tells us that our true reality is not a limited phenomenon, holding on to an isolated and vulnerable existence between the point of birth and death, but eternal life that exists alone, self-existent, and self-sufficient, the essence of all that is, was, and ever will be throughout the universe.

That is what you really are.

I am not sure you are ready to accept this answer. If you do, it will be one of the biggest wake-up calls in your life. This is the heart of the teaching of Tao, and it is what I realized through direct experience and reflection on the nature of life. With this realization, things are restored to their proper places, permanence as permanence and impermanence as impermanence.

Below is a poem that I dedicated to my students, celebrating the life that connects all of us in a circle.

POEM OF LIFE

Sensing mystery
From whence did life come?
The flame of life
Bright and beautiful
Too large for the human vessel.

Sea of life
Hills and valleys of life
Sky of life
The flickering glow of the firefly

Sings of mystery
Indefinable.

What is reality?
Do you know?
The firefly's sparkling flash
Moment to moment
Into eternity
Exists life, life!

THE FOUNDATION FOR CHANGE

Do you like changes? Or are they stressors to you? Are you excited about change? Or are you afraid?

We have a basic, instinctive desire for safety and security, and change, while bringing opportunities, also entails risk. We may lose what we have now. This makes many of us afraid of and resistant to change, and hesitant to initiate changes that require us to take action and do something. This is especially true now, because the scope of the changes that we need to create goes far beyond our personal lives. Thoughts, beliefs, behaviors, habits, lifestyles, cultures, and systems—all of these must undergo deep and far-reaching transformation.

What is the master key to all these changes? What makes all these changes possible? Where do we find the courage, power, and wisdom to create the changes we want to see in the world?

As I mentioned in the Introduction, from my own experience, I realized that the confidence, power, and wisdom to create changes in our life come from knowing what we really are, from knowing our changeless nature.

Behind our behaviors are our beliefs, which determine how we think things are and what we conceive to be possible and on a broader scale. The foundation of all these beliefs is our conception of who we are, whether we are conscious of it or not.

As I described in the discussion about the transition from the eye of Ego to the eye of Tao, most people today believe that we are a solid entity separate from other beings in the world. We don't question this belief because it is based on a perception that we have repeatedly verified throughout our lives. Even right at this moment, you can verify it by hitting the wall with your fist. The thing that hurts is your hand, and the thing that doesn't is the wall. How can anyone with common sense doubt this obvious truth?

However, questioning this belief is the beginning of our journey to find who or what we really are. We will challenge this long-held belief and examine its source, which will help us remove our narrowly focused glasses and see things in a more holistic and balanced perspective. Through this journey, we seek to find something unchanging within us, which I believe will guide us not only through the changes and transformations we desire and dream about but also toward the complete realization of our true potential as individuals and as humanity.

Our guide on this journey of discovery will be the pioneering spirit of modern science, proceeding hand in hand with the most cherished spiritual traditions of humanity.

CHAPTER TWO

What Are We Really?

WE ARE CURIOUS

Curiosity is part of human nature. We ask questions and want to know about things, how they work, where they come from. I do. Don't you? The end of this curiosity and questioning is knowing the origin of being, my being, and the being of the universe.

Who am I? Why am I here? As we developed the notion of *I*, we asked our parents and other grown-ups such questions and had to be content with not very convincing answers. While looking up into the sky on starry nights, we wondered how those countless stars came to exist and how they happened to be so twinkly. We also wanted to know where the sky ended and what lay beyond its end.

These are the questions that were asked not only by us, but also by generations of people since the dawn of our civilization. Humanity has tried to quench this thirst for knowing in two main ways: by externally observing and analyzing the objective world around us, and by looking within, internally examining what's happening in one's mind, and trying to understand.

The objective, analytic investigation of the external world led to the development of science and technology. The subjective, contemplative exploration brought wisdom and insights that provided the source of inspiration for diverse spiritual-religious traditions. What is extremely fascinating is that in our time, these two approaches have become very close to each other, to the point that they both seem to be saying the same thing about some of the most fundamental questions about life.

To find out what we really are, we can do what scientists do: Begin on the surface and probe more deeply into nature. We can start from what we see, feel, and touch, and proceed down to deeper and subtler layers of our being.

THERE IS MORE TO LIFE

We are all organisms, and we have organs. Organs are made of tissues, and tissues consist of cells. So far, so good. However, even at the level of cells, our conventional belief about reality begins to be challenged.

As we know, a cell is the fundamental unit of a living organism. Each of us started from a single cell that multiplied by dividing itself. Through the recent advancement of genetic technology, we have become able to develop a whole organism not only from a stem cell, but also from a normal somatic cell. This is possible because each cell has its own independent mechanism of life, and contains within itself the information and potential to become a whole organism, as an acorn contains the potential to become a giant oak tree.

We don't yet know exactly how each cell regulates its behavior and collaborates with other cells in a multicellular organism. It seems that these cells voluntarily regulate themselves like people who have gathered together to do something greater than they can do individually. But at the same time, they seem to have the capacity to choose their own path instead of working with others for a common good, which is the case for a cancer cell.

If these cells, while forming a bigger organism, are themselves independent organisms that work together voluntarily, we may wonder where *I* begins to exist. Where does this collection of independent organisms begin to be me? Is *I* a real entity or is it just a concept for convenience to label the collection of all the constituents that work together for a common good?

We can apply the same thought to all constituents of me other than the cells of my body. If we look into what we mean by *me*, we can see lots of *mine*'s. My body, gender, age, name, job, family, home, computers, cars, memory, money, Facebook page, personal relationships and social networks. None of these are *me*. They are mine. None of them feel like me.

Here's an exercise that I would propose: Select any of the items on that list and ask yourself, "Do I stop being me if this is removed?" Will you cease to be you without your computer?

What about your home? Your name? If your answer is no, meaning that you continue to be you even if the particular item is removed, you can disqualify it as a definitive constituent of who you are. Go through the whole list in the same way, and see what is left. My guess is that you will end up with nothing that qualifies. Even your body doesn't qualify because the body alone doesn't make a person a person.

Then where is it? Is *me* a reality or just a label, like a folder name, which doesn't have any real content by itself but just refers to a collection of related files? When we ask, "Who am I?" are we chasing a ghost that actually doesn't exist? What makes *me*? Maybe the most likely candidate is the essential life force, whatever that is, because when it leaves the body, people think you have ceased to exist.

It is too soon to have any definitive answer at this point, but trying to stay open and seeing with fresh eyes will be important.

If we go deeper, past cells to the levels of molecules and atoms, the situation becomes more confusing. At the level of atoms, all the value judgments that you have held in your life, and which we all tend to take seriously in terms of our identity and self-definition and how we see others—things like good and bad, beautiful and ugly, right and wrong, clean and dirty—all begin to dissolve. There can be some molecules with abnormal or distorted structures. However, there is no such thing as a "bad" atom! At the level of atoms, all biological and chemical attributes such as tastes and smells, are not found: they are properties of molecules.

Also, many of the physical attributes such as colors and sounds are not present because—so I am told by brilliant scientific minds—these attributes do not come directly from atoms but from the mathematical and structural relations that an atom forms with other atoms. All atoms, even the atoms that make up something that you think is the most horrible, the ugliest, and the nastiest thing in the world, show the dynamic balance, order, and harmony present throughout the universe.

It is only a matter of the depth of observation.

Up to this point, things still look pretty solid. But when we go beyond the level of atoms, the landscape changes dramatically. Let's go a little deeper into an atom. Let's use a hydrogen atom because it has the simplest structure, just a single electron and a single proton. If you expand a hydrogen atom to the size of a football field, the nucleus in the middle of the atom is about the size of your thumbnail, or you can imagine it as a ping-pong ball. Can you see that image, a tiny white ping-pong ball at the center of a 100-yard-long football field? What is between the nucleus and the outer boundary of the atom? Space.

That hydrogen atom—as every atom—is about 99.99999… percent space. Physically, as a body, you are virtually empty. Or put another way: you are virtually not there!

The theory of relativity tells us that matter and energy are equivalent and interchangeable. Basically, matter is contained or frozen energy. If you go one step further below the atom, to the subatomic or quantum universe, the distinction between matter and energy disappears and you become 100 percent space, with nothing solid in it. There are no parts and no separations anymore. There's only one space, one energy, and one universe. Sound too empty? Don't worry. As you will find out, it is not just a void.

Now get ready for some increased weirdness. Although

quantum mechanics is considered the most successful theory ever devised to explain the world, and its applications to technology such as lasers, transistors, medical imaging technology, CDs, and DVDs are almost too many to enumerate, its principles are strange indeed.

Niels Bohr, the Nobel Prize–winning Danish physicist who was one of the founders of quantum theory, said, "Anyone who is not shocked by quantum theory has not understood it." And Richard Feynman of Cal Tech, another Nobel Prize winner and one of the greatest mathematicians and physicists of the 20th century, said, "I think I can safely say that nobody understands quantum mechanics." So don't worry if some of what I'm going to talk about now is difficult to grasp; just keep open and stay with me.

In a famous experiment known as the double-slit experiment, scientists shot electrons through two vertical slits, which hit against a screen. One would expect the marks left by the electrons to form a pattern of two lines, as would happen if we threw little pebbles against a wall through two vertical windows. However, the particles, even when shot through one at a time, formed an interference pattern rather than lines. This is what would happen if we sent a *wave* through the slits, not a particle. The particles appeared to go through *both* slits like a wave. How could it be that a single particle could act as a wave and go through both slits at the same time?

To determine which slit the electrons were passing through, the researchers added a detector next to each slit. Amazingly, when the measurements from the detectors were gathered, the interference pattern was gone, and a pattern indicative of particles, not waves, was revealed.

It didn't make sense that something could be a wave, fluid and boundless, and at precisely the same time, be a particle, definite and solid. And how could observation by a conscious mind, nonmaterial and at a distance, make changes in the state of an objective physical reality? You might argue that what was observing was a mechanism, which hardly deserves to be called a conscious mind. But who designed the device? Who put it there? Who interpreted the data? Conscious minds.

Because the researchers could not believe their findings, they assumed there had been a measurement problem and performed the experiment repeatedly, always ending up with the same results. The conclusion: quantum phenomena can and do behave as both particles and waves. In physics, this is known as the wave-particle duality and is a fundamental principle of quantum mechanics. At the quantum level, all matter exhibits properties of both particles and waves. Indeed, one prominent scientist proposed calling it a *wavicle*.

The most widely accepted interpretation of this phenomenon is that on the quantum level, what exists are *waves of probabilities*, which manifest as a physical reality through observation by a conscious mind. Einstein, unable to accept this interpretation, said, "How can I believe the moon doesn't exist unless I am looking at it?" He struggled with this idea throughout his life.

But the principle was validated repeatedly through observation. So, how can we answer the question that Einstein raised? It seems the only reasonable explanation is that the moon—and everything else—is being observed all the time. But if not by you or by me, then by whom?

Because the implications of these discoveries are so profound, let me reiterate the main points before we move on: At the subatomic level, what looks like a solid structure on grosser, more manifest levels dissolves into waves of probabilities. A probability wave is not a thing like a grain of sand or a pebble. It is not material. What this means is that, in the investigation of matter, physics has discovered that the most subtle, elemental unit of "matter" is not material at all!

These probabilities turn into physical reality through observation by a conscious mind. Nonmaterial probabilities become material objects through observation, which means your conscious mind creates physical reality! Where the mathematical probabilities collapse into a physical reality (object), there is always the observing consciousness (subject). Subject works together with object in creating a phenomenon; or in other words, subject is not separate from object.

"We are not simply bystanders on a cosmic stage," said Princeton University physicist John Wheeler, "we are shapers and creators living in a participatory universe." Because big things are made of small things, these conclusions of quantum physics apply not only to subatomic particles but also to big, macroscopic objects such as you, me, and everything else.

This understanding, instead of answering our inquiries, raises more questions about what we really are.

If observation by a conscious mind is required for probability waves to turn into physical reality, and this principle applies not only to small particles but also to big things including the universe itself, we have to wonder what kind of conscious observation caused this universe to take form as a physical reality from a mere probability, and to maintain continuity in its inexplicably intricate order and harmony. And how did it happen at the very beginning, when there were no physicists, no sentient beings, and no life at all to observe the formation of the galaxies and stars?

Look around: your car, your house, the mountain behind your house, the sky and the countless stars sprinkled on it, and yourself. How is my breath being breathed, and how does my heart keep beating? While you are sleeping, who is watching you to make sure you continue to exist as a physical reality? How is the sun aflame so brightly and warmly without skipping even a single day in billions of years? What unimaginably imperturbable observer is watching over all of these to make sure everything works? It is truly a mystery.

One thing we need to understand is that *watching* doesn't necessarily mean seeing through eyes. (We cannot see the particles anyway; they are far too small.) What it actually means is "knowing," or "being aware." So the subject, the watcher, doesn't need to have eyes. But it has to be aware.

If you think you have not been watching your life and didn't do much to maintain your reality, this principle of quantum mechanics would suggest that you need to be deeply grateful that you are still here! To whom? To what awareness? We are not sure yet.

ENERGY AND CONSCIOUSNESS

Through the findings of modern physics, such as the theory of relativity and quantum mechanics, we now understand the duality of matter-energy, time-space, and particle-wave: that matter and energy are interchangeable; that time and space are relative and connected; and that quantum events have the attributes of both particles and waves.

One important relationship science has not yet resolved is between energy and consciousness. We do know that consciousness, which used to be considered a property or product of the individual brain of a sentient being, is involved in the manifestation of physical reality in the universe. Even though we don't know how consciousness exists or how it is woven into the fabric of the universe, it seems we cannot avoid consciousness if we are to explain physical reality in an integrative way.

The two primary aspects or components of reality that the universe reveals to us through these discoveries are Energy and Consciousness. All other things that are found in the universe can be understood as manifestations of these two fundamentals.

There are historical views that see these two as one. In the Eastern tradition, energy and consciousness are viewed as different aspects of the same thing. In this tradition, energy is understood to be the origin and reality of the universe. As seen in the ancient Taoist principle that mind creates energy and energy creates mind, energy and mind are viewed as one inseparable entity. Energy and mind, while changing to each other and producing limitlessly diverse phenomena, are ultimately one.

The Vedic tradition of India teaches the same principle,

using different terminology: silence and dynamism are together forever. *Shiva* (silence, unbounded pure consciousness) and *Shakti* (dynamism, creativity) are always united in a cosmic embrace of wholeness that creates and sustains the world.

The unity of Energy-Consciousness is also what I realized to be the true reality through my own contemplative investigation. From the time I was a young boy, "Who am I?" was the biggest enigma for me, and the desire to know the answer was my greatest desire. That I don't know the answer to this question made me suspicious of all others that I perceived and experienced. How can a being who doesn't know who he/she/it is know about anything else? It is really a case of "What the bleep do I know?" Because the desire for the answer to this question was compelling, I found it extremely difficult to get used to the norm of life in school and in society.

When I was not able to escape from this question any longer, I went to a sacred mountain in Korea, after making minimal arrangements for my wife and two sons' living, for a meditation without eating or sleeping for 21 days. Even though I didn't tell my wife and sons, I knew I would not come back if I didn't get the answer—or perhaps I should say, *until* I got the answer. I was that desperate and determined.

When I thought I had done everything that I could do, and with an extreme pain in my head, I finally let go of all my remaining desire to live. At that moment, I experienced an explosion in my brain that was so intense I had to touch my head to determine whether it was still there: my awareness felt so open that I thought my head had been blown away.

With the explosion, all pain was gone, and everything

became clear. In the absolute quietude and clarity, I could see what I really am. At the moment of awakening, the answer I had been seeking and longing for was obvious, compelling, and indisputable: "The cosmic energy is my energy and my energy is the cosmic energy. The cosmic mind is my mind, and my mind is the cosmic mind."

I realized that the reality of the universe is Energy-Consciousness, and it is also what I am. It was a direct seeing or knowing, not learning. It just is, and that is what I truly am. This unity doesn't have any shape or borders, and is not bound by time and space. Paradoxically, the closest word that we can find in our language to describe this enormously great, infinitely powerful, all-knowing Reality that creates, sustains, and regulates the cosmos is: Nothing. It is not a thing nor an object. It has no qualities or characteristics. It is the unmanifested source of all, pure Being, One-without-a-second.

NOTHING, AND SOMETHING FROM NOTHING

Nothing, as the ultimate reality and the source of the unity of energy and consciousness, is not only my personal realization of what I really am, but also the essential teaching of the Korean tradition of Tao, to which I am culturally indebted. To give proper credit to this great body of knowledge, I would like to explain its core principles briefly.

The most ancient scripture of Korean Taoism is *Chun-BuKyung*. The title can be translated as "Scripture of Heavenly

Code." It consists of 81 characters that start from *Il* (One) and end with the same character *Il* (One), forming a perfect symmetric balance of nine by nine, and a complete cycle of one to one.

The first characters are *Il-Shi-Mu-Shi*. In letter-to-letter translation, that is one-begin-no-begin. This can be interpreted as "One begins that has no beginning." The scripture ends with *Il-Jong-Mu-Jong-Il*, which is translated to one-end-no-end-one, meaning "One ends, but there's no end to One."

Another five characters that deliver the key message of this scripture are, *In-Jung-Chun-Ji-Il*. This is translated literally as human-inside-heaven-earth-one, which means "Human has heaven and earth as one." These characters tell us that inside the human, the three elements of heaven, earth, and human exist as a unity. In the traditional understanding of Korean Taoism, Heaven represents the laws of the universe, Earth represents substance, and Human represents possibilities of creation, life force, or conscious mind.

So the whole 81 characters can be summarized into 14 characters: *Il-Shi-Mu-Shi, Il-Jong-Mu-Jong-Il, In-Jung-Chun-Ji-Il.* These 14 characters can be recapitulated into three characters: *Chun-Ji-In*, Heaven-Earth-Human. Finally these three characters can be condensed into one character, which is *Il,* One, which is the ultimate reality.

If we were asked to visualize this One, we would probably imagine one object positioned on a plain background, like a circle on a white board. This is because we, being so accustomed to living among objects in a material world, are too attached to things or beings. However, this is not the true One yet. Because of the distinction of inside and outside, there's already duality involved.

Then, what do you need to do to attain one? Good guess! You have to remove the line of the circle. Then there's no "object." And because there's no object, there's now no "background." It is Nothing. That is the true One. Therefore, in the context of this scripture, One and Nothing are identical.

Because of its own infinite nature, Nothing has no beginning or end. Because it doesn't have size, it is bigger than the biggest thing, and smaller than the smallest. Nothing cannot be reached by looking into deep space or traveling to the ends of the known universe. Nothing is behind, around, and within all that exists. To make a distinction between Nothing, which is not visible but has all power to create everything, and a mere absence of things, we also call Nothing the True Void.

According to the discoveries of modern cosmology, we cannot explain the movement of a galaxy by the total mass of all the observed matter in it. The observed matter is simply not enough. Mathematically, there should be more matter, but we haven't located it yet. Because it is not visible, scientists call this unobserved matter *dark matter*.

There's more. Scientists figured out how to calculate the energy and matter of the entire universe, but the total energy and matter, observable whether directly or indirectly, cannot explain the way the universe looks. For the universe to look the way it does, there should be more energy in the space between galaxies, which looks completely empty. More energy is there but we cannot see it. Because it is not observed yet, it is called *dark energy*.

All observable energy and matter is calculated to constitute only 5 percent of the total energy and matter of the universe.

Ninety-five percent of the universe is not observable. The search for dark matter and dark energy is one of the hottest pursuits in modern science.

Why am I telling you this? Because, as a way to explain this "darkness," or invisibility, of the universe, Nothing, or the potential of empty space, has been strongly suggested. And this is not merely a fanciful idea. As it turns out, empty space has been discovered to be a very different kind of Nothing than anyone expected. It is "no thing," but it is fluctuating with enormous potential energy from which it is able to generate particles; that is, "something." Or, more truly, *everything*. In this way, physics has drawn ever closer to the insights of ancient seers who saw the great Void, the Nothing, the One, in their deep meditations.

In modern physics, Nothing, with its inherent quantum fluctuation, is suggested as one of the most likely candidates that can explain the beginning of the universe and the existence of something rather than nothing.

From the standpoint of physics, 1) Nothing contains, and is, the infinite creative potential of the energy-matter of the entire universe; 2) inherent within this unbounded, unmanifested Reality, are all the possibilities for all the objects and all their possible interactions throughout the universe; and 3) The universal laws that all these possibilities will follow in order to manifest as phenomena.

Do you see how these three correspond to the three fundamentals of Tao: Heaven (laws), Earth (substance) and Human (life as creative force)? These also can be explained as the Three Virtues of Tao: Possibilities as Great Compassion in the sense that it allows and supports all life-forms and all beings to be what they choose to be without judgment; Laws as Great Wisdom in the sense that it knows how everything works; and Nothing as Great Power in the sense that it has the capacity to generate all the energy and matter of the entire universe.

These three are one in Tao, which by its own nature is timeless. For some reason that we don't know, the Possibilities began to manifest by using the resources of Nothing, according to the Laws. That was the beginning of our time.

Nothing is the universe's great storehouse and power plant. Laws give the universe order and stability, while possibilities give the universe dynamic creativity and change. Through the balance of these, the universe maintains its eternal dynamic harmony that provides all beings with the environment in which they can realize their potential value. This is the picture of the world that Tao presents to us.

WHAT DOES NOTHING MEAN TO ME?

Can you come up with any word in English that has all these meanings, all possibilities (Great Compassion), the universal laws (Great Wisdom), and the potential of the energy and matter of the entire universe (Great Power)? The word that I can find is God, with its implication of omniscience and omnipotence, when we remove all religious and denominational attributes from the meaning.

In the Korean language, the pronunciation of the word for One is *Hana*. And we use *Nim* as a suffix to refer to someone or something respectfully. If you combine Hana (One) and Nim, it forms another independent word, different from Hana. Can you guess the meaning of *Hananim* in Korean? Good guess. It is "God." Hananim is the exact translation of God in Korean.

With the question "What are we really?" in mind, we have traveled a long way in this chapter, stopping to consider many fascinating topics, including the essential teachings of Tao, ancient scriptures, and some basic discoveries of modern physics (with my humble apology for my very limited understanding). I hope the journey was fun and useful to you, and here's what we have reached: the unity of energy and consciousness, Tao, One, Nothing, and Hananim (God) are all the same, and that's what we really are.

If we truly accept this, our perceptions and our behavior are bound to undergo some profound changes. First of all, we will recognize the manifestation or expression of this oneness in everyone and everything we get in touch with. Appreciating that this oneness is the divine creative power and life of the universe, moving and breathing in the people we meet and the objects we encounter, we will spontaneously treat everyone and everything with respect, and what Buddhists call "loving kindness." Based on the acceptance and acknowledgement of this ultimate commonality, compassion will arise naturally.

Compassion is different from pity. Pity is based on comparison and difference, the unconscious thought that "I am in a better position than the other." Compassion, on the other hand, is based on recognition of commonality. "You are just like me, and that's why I can feel how you feel." When we acknowledge this ultimate commonality, in any action we take toward others, no harm will ever be intended. From the acknowledgment of this oneness, which encompasses everything in a great circle of life, our primary attitude toward other people and other life-forms will be to bring benefit to others. And we will discover that because of the intimate interconnectedness of all life, benefiting others is also benefiting ourselves.

Even though from one perspective we can say having this attitude is a great spiritual achievement, what it really takes is only the willingness to accept the truth that reveals itself to pure observation. That's the ultimate message of the spirit of Tao: know what you really are, and widely benefit all. That was also exactly what I realized through meditation and practice.

Even when we have realized oneness and nothingness, we still have our personal lives to manage, bodies to take care of, and mouths to feed, and you will know which one is yours and which ones are others', so you won't put food into another person's mouth when you are hungry. Also you won't kiss a rattlesnake or hug a cactus no matter how strong an affinity you feel toward them. But at the same time, we know these apparent separations are functional, not fundamental, and should be recognized as such without mistaking one for the other. I would call this apparent separation "functional ego," or you can call it your "character," which is the collection of your beliefs, habits, and other people's expectations.

Can you maintain the awareness of ultimate commonality while you are fully engaged in your life as a functional ego or a character? I believe you can, and this can be a powerful spiritual practice for anyone. This practice will continue until the gap between those two, your true nature and your character, is filled, and your character manifests your true nature completely. My guess is that you will find the gap to be very enjoyable to fill.

CHAPTER THREE

LifeParticles

PROPOSING LIFEPARTICLES

It may be useful for us to have a single name that can refer to the unity of energy and consciousness. We can combine those terms as Energy-Consciousness, which works. But the term I propose is *LifeParticles*. In this chapter I will explain why I believe this is an appropriate term, consistent with the knowledge coming to us from spiritual traditions and modern science.

From the observations in the previous chapter, the attributes of LifeParticles can be inferred as follows:

1. They are "particles" of the unity of Energy-Consciousness, which I have also referred to as Nothing.
2. As particles of Nothing, they don't have mass, charge,

or extension (size); and therefore, are not bound by time and space. This means they can reach anywhere instantly without limitation.

3. They exist both as particles and as one great unbroken whole, because there's no distinction between parts and the whole in Nothing.

One of the reasons I propose to call this ultimate substance LifeParticles relates to the core of the phenomenon of life. Life, like consciousness, is one of the mysteries of the universe that humanity has sought to understand. We have attained a fairly detailed understanding about how a living system works in organisms of various degrees of complexity. But we don't have any idea how the fire of life itself is sparked or where it comes from.

What constitutes life? We use the term *organism* to refer to an organic entity that displays the functions of living things. In addition to this functional term, we use the word *sentient* to refer to an essential aspect of life. Sentient beings are beings that have the capability to feel or more simply, have consciousness. In other words, being sentient, which is one of the most definitive characteristics of life, involves both energy and consciousness—or we can describe it as "energy that has consciousness." In its most fundamental sense, the phenomenon of life is a combination of energy and consciousness.

Life understood this way goes beyond the understanding of the phenomenon of life as a biological process in a living organism. The phenomenon of life as a biological process is maintained and observed only down to the cellular level of an organism, but the organization of matter and energy, the foundation of the life phenomenon, doesn't stop at the level of cells. If we go down deeper to the levels of molecules and atoms, the distinction that is probably the most vital distinction in our life, between "alive" and "dead," disappears.

In an effort to see the process of life from the deeper level of reality, many explanations of the process of life from the level of molecules, atoms, and even from the quantum level are offered in modern science. Even though we are far from a theory that can consistently and comprehensively explain the organization of matter and energy from the subatomic level up to the highest level of mental or spiritual activities in the human brain, it is obvious that essentially the same energy flows throughout the process of life at all levels.

Life in the context of the teaching of Tao, which I also follow in this book, refers to this flow of energy rather than the biological process in a particular organism. Based on this broader and more fundamental view of life, and the direct association between the phenomenon of life and the unity of energy and consciousness, I propose to call the particles of energy and consciousness LifeParticles.

Eastern culture has held this view for thousands of years, built theories to understand the human body energetically, and developed intricate methodologies to heal the system and maintain its healthy balance by strengthening and directing the energy. In East Asia, foundation of this energy system in the human body is explained as the meridian system of subtle channels through which the energy flows—*dahnjons*, or energy centers—and acupuncture points where the energy can be most easily influenced.

In India, exactly parallel to this system are the *nadis*, or channels; *chakras*, or energy centers; and *marma* points, which are equivalent to acupuncture points and usually located in exactly the same place on the body. The terminology is somewhat different, but both the Indian and the East Asian energy systems are based on the understanding that the universe consists of Consciousness-Energy that creates the phenomenon of life when it flows through an organic system.

Even though we use the term *energy*, it doesn't belong to any of the categories of forces that are currently known and measurable in physical science. However, the known universe is vastly less than the unknown. As was discussed in the previous chapter, the observable matter and energy is only about 5 percent of the universe.

On the other hand, this subtle energy, even though unobserved by physical science, integrated with the mind in an inseparable unity, has been utilized in, for example, martial arts and medicine, with enormous practical benefits for thousands of years. So it will be reasonable to be open to this new idea of reality, the unity of Energy-Consciousness, which I call LifeParticles.

I believe the study of LifeParticles will be one of the most fertile areas of future research. It will produce profound discoveries and facilitate our understanding about life and the nature of the universe, as well as a deeper understanding of who we most truly are.

WHAT MAKES AN EXPERIENCE AN EXPERIENCE?

I live in Sedona, a small town in northern Arizona well known for the majestic beauty of its ancient and towering red-rock formations. Sedona has many other marvelous attractions. One of them is the desert sunset, ever-changing in its beauty. The combinations of blue, orange, crimson, and violet create an indescribable palette of colors. But what makes the experience of Sedona's sunsets unique and awe inspiring is not simply the ever-varied colors. It is your presence, and your consciousness, that make the experience so powerful. Depending on your degree of wakefulness, the depth and fullness of the experience will vary. The electromagnetic waves containing the range of frequencies that could be viewed as blue, orange, crimson, or violet are there. But it is your wakeful presence in awareness that interacts with these waves and turns them into an experience of breathtaking beauty.

What exactly is experienced at that moment? It is the totality of the impressions that all things present there leave on your perception. In modern philosophy, this is called *qualia*. Qualia is the essence of an experience, the essence of knowing. It is the taste of a peach, the heat of fire. No matter how much you read about water, for example, no matter how much you intellectually understand the physical and chemical properties of water, you will never know what water is until you drink it or put your hands into it to feel it. You are not drinking the idea of water or the description of water. You are drinking the reality of water. The qualia that you experience varies depending on your physical, mental, and emotional conditions, in conjunction with the physical and chemical properties of the water at the very moment.

This experience—and in fact, any experience—as the totality of the influences of all of these factors on your perception, is unique: it will occur only once in your lifetime and only once in the entire history of the universe, because all the factors existing and interacting in that moment were participating with their unique vibrations, which change all the time. All of these, including the totality of your life experiences culminating in the present moment of awareness, combined to create the experience of the moment, whether it is viewing the sunset in Sedona, walking barefoot through the shallow water in Oak Creek Canyon, riding the subway in New York, or strolling with a loved one along the Cheonggyecheon River in downtown Seoul.

Language, concepts, names, and digitized information are replicable, but the qualia of an experience isn't. This applies not only to the sunset view that touched my heart at a specific moment on a particular date, but also to all experiences, small or large, simple or profound. Right at this moment, the moment you become aware of yourself, you can feel the presence of the things around you, including the space. That experience doesn't come from any understanding, knowledge, intellectual analysis, or interpretation. It comes directly from being present with all things in the living moment, the Now. In that experience of being present, there's no separation between you and other things. If you feel a separation, you are already out of the present, and have gone into your comfortable and familiar land of names and concepts.

IF A TREE FALLS IN A FOREST
WHEN NOBODY IS AROUND . . .

Where does this experience occur? How does it happen? Is it in your senses, or your brain, is it in space, at the boundary of your body, or in things around you? Where does the experience come from? This reminds me of the age-old question: "If a tree falls in the forest, and nobody is there to hear it, does it make a sound?" If we don't think about it at all, we may shoot back an answer quickly and decisively: "Of course, it does," even with a hint that this question is too dumb to bother answering. This reflects our firm belief in an objective reality that exists independently of our perception.

But what we perceive as sound are actually pulses of air in general or in the case of the falling tree, the rapid vibrations of air caused by the trunk of the tree violently striking the ground. When the pulse happens within the specific frequency range of 20 to 20,000 times a second (20 to 20,000 Hz), it will stimulate the nerves in our ear, and when the signals are caught by our brain, we experience the vibration as sound. If the vibration is below or above this range, it is the same vibrating air, but it doesn't generate the experience of hearing sound. This means you or anybody with ears and a brain are an indispensable constituent in creating the perceptual experience of sound. A tree that falls in a forest when nobody is there creates only air pulses with no sound.

The same explanation applies to visual perception, such as the magnificent sunset of Sedona I described before. Just as in the case of sound, we take this experience of visual perception so for granted that we rarely ask what constituents are involved in it. The sun, of course. What else? Your eyes, which catch the electromagnetic waves between 400 and 700 nanometers in length, and only within that range. Electromagnetic waves beyond this very limited range, even though they are the same kind of electromagnetic waves by nature, won't be experienced as light of any kind, much less as the rich mixture of the various hues of the desert sunset in Sedona. What would happen if the tree fell, and the potential observer, with perfectly functioning ears, eyes, and brain, was there but unconscious at exactly that moment? Ears can sense the vibration and send the signals to the brain. The brain can process the signal, but when you are unconscious, it is not registered in your mind and no experience happens. This observation gives us a strong hint about where the experience occurs, and how.

Scientists in the modern era are not the only ones who have analyzed the mechanics of experience. Spiritual teachers, from the time of Buddha and before, have pointed out to their disciples that it is not our eyes that see or our ears that hear; rather, it is our consciousness that sees, hears, tastes, smells, and feels through the mechanism of the senses. Indian philosophy speaks of the invisible experiencer within as the "dweller in the body." When you paint your house with music playing while you work, you wouldn't say that the house sees the new colors or hears the music, but rather it is the dweller in the house who brings a lively, living consciousness.

The common factor in all our experiences, regardless of kind, is consciousness, or more precisely, wakeful consciousness. This applies to all experiences. What *happens* doesn't form an experience. It is our wakeful consciousness or awareness that turns what happens into an experience or a meaningful reality. It sounds like a parallel of the statement of quantum physics: the waves of probabilities collapse into a physical reality through observation by a conscious mind. This means that what underlies everything that happens, ranging from an impersonal physical reality (outside your brain) to a personal subjective experience (inside your brain), is consciousness.

Ultimately, it is not *my* consciousness or *your* consciousness that experiences and perceives, but consciousness itself. Here is a poem I wrote one night to share what I realized from my reflection on the nature of consciousness:

DIVINITY

A night deep in darkness
A bright star came into my brain
and whispered in my ears
The twinkling stars you see above
It is your eyes that see them
The raindrops hitting against the windows
It is your ears that hear them

I had thought
That it was I who saw the stars
that it was I who heard the rain

Now that I open my eyes and ears anew

I realize that I am the stars and the rain

A bright light shines one more time
Then I am neither the star nor the rain
Truly realizing myself and all,
I am eternal life that exists alone and on its own

Stars continue to twinkle and
raindrops just continue to fall

WHAT IS CONSCIOUSNESS?

Quantum physics tells us that observation by conscious mind is
needed to turn probabilities into physical reality. Only a conscious mind can do this, not a machine. Of course, a machine
can be used to make measurements and record data, but there
must also be a mind that uses the machine as an instrument of
observation, a mind to interpret the information. Even though
this is still being debated and many different experimental
designs have been utilized in the attempt to determine exactly
what qualifies as conscious observation, all experiments to test
whether machines can have the same effect suggest the same
conclusion: technology alone doesn't produce the result of physical manifestation.

Let's look further into the meaning of this discovery.
You are at point A and you observe an object at point B. Your
consciousness at point A creates material changes in the object

that is at point B. It is magic! It must be—otherwise, how can something at one location have physical effects at another location without any known connecting force or energy between the two locations, such as gravity, magnetism, electricity, radiation or any other force known to science? None of these apply to consciousness because it doesn't have mass; it doesn't have size or extension; it is not magnetic or electrical.

What is the nature of consciousness that can be inferred from this observation?

1. Consciousness exists. Otherwise, how do we know that we exist?
2. Consciousness is not confined within an individual brain. Otherwise, how can it cause changes in the physical state of things outside the brain?
3. Consciousness is not bound by time and space since its essential component or constituent doesn't have any mass, charge, or extension. Otherwise, we should be able to measure its weight and size.
4. Consciousness can travel through space or can be present at multiple locations simultaneously. Otherwise, we cannot explain how a conscious mind here can create a material change there. Logically, there's no reason why consciousness can't travel infinitely fast or be omnipresent, because having no mass, charge, and extension, it won't be limited by time and space or by any other known physical forces.
5. Consciousness has power to create physical changes. Interestingly, in physical science, energy is defined as

the capacity to perform work. Work may mean stress or joy to you, but in a purely physical sense, work means creating changes in a physical state. This means that consciousness, since it can and does create changes in the state of an objective physical reality, must have the property of energy. Because consciousness doesn't use any medium other than itself to work, it not only has the property of energy, but also should be energy itself. And because the creation of physical reality through conscious observation should apply to the universe itself—for the manifestation of the physical, material universe—consciousness must exist throughout the universe or have the capacity to reach the entire universe. From this observation, we can reasonably infer that not only is consciousness energy but that it is also the very nature of the universe.

Thanks to the theory of relativity and observations that validated the theory, we already know that matter and energy are equivalent and interchangeable. Even empty space is not that empty, as we've discussed. Empty space is known to be full of energy that is fluctuating ceaselessly. Energy is everywhere.

For me, all of this serves to corroborate the insights I had in my moment of self-realization and thereafter: that the unity of Energy-Consciousness is the ultimate reality. Because consciousness doesn't have mass and extension, has no parts or physical properties, it is Nothing, which, on the other hand, can generate the matter and energy of the entire universe. Nothing, energy, and consciousness fit well together because they are one and the same. LifeParticle is the name that I've proposed to refer to both the tiniest, infinitesimal units and the whole of this unity. LifeParticles are the particles of Nothingness that have attributes of both being and nonbeing, and the particles of energy and consciousness, which are the essence of Life.

We don't yet know how to validate this through observation, because these are currently unobservable by any known method of measurement. But as we have done many times before in human history, I believe we will figure out how to verify whether this is a truthful description of reality or not. It may take time and require some changes in our beliefs, perspectives, and attitudes, because people have a hard time working with a new paradigm in which they do not yet believe.

A perfect example is quantum mechanics, which has been called the most perfect theory ever devised, and which is at the basis of the invention of thousands of products and technologies. And yet most people—including scientists, it must be said—have a difficult time understanding and accepting it.

Nevertheless, I believe that the study of what I am calling LifeParticles will be the most prolific area in the pursuit of truth, whether by subjective and contemplative means or by the objective and analytic methodologies of science, as we begin to recognize the central importance of this notion—the unity of energy and consciousness—in understanding truth.

MORE THAN KI, OR QI

Energy is not a new idea conceived by modern science. In the tradition of Tao, it was The Reality, the manifestation of Tao itself. Energy, or really, the unity or wholeness of Energy-Consciousness, as previously discussed, was believed to be the force that creates and underlies all phenomena on all levels of being—physical, mental, and spiritual.

However, this original understanding faded as people became more interested in material living and practical uses of energy. Since then, energy—which came to be known as *Ki*, or *Qi*—has been studied mostly for improving health and to increase longevity. Some practitioners believed that they could even achieve immortality. Through studies and empirical tests, an intricate system of diagnosis and healing was developed. In our era, study and application of Ki does not ordinarily extend farther than the doorways of practitioners of Oriental Medicine or the studios of martial artists and their students.

However, discussing these important but limited uses of Ki is not my intention. I am proposing the unity of Energy-Consciousness with all its implications as the fundamental reality of life, and thereby, of course, the fundamental reality of ourselves.

As I have written about elsewhere, when I was a boy and a young man, I sought to know what the true essence of my existence was. After a long and arduous process, I found that it was Cosmic Energy (*Chunjigiun*) and Cosmic Mind (*Chunji-maeum*). And energy and consciousness were not separate. Each was the action of the other. Energy creates Mind, and Mind creates Energy.

I realized that the energy that animated my body was the same energy that flowed through the cosmos. I also realized that our minds and consciousness were connected to everything else in the cosmos through this flow of energy. For me, this did not and does not need any explanation because that's the reality I experienced. I am that. However, I was not satisfied with this state of "knowing" alone. I wanted a proof that my knowing was a true one. I wanted to test it against reality, to verify it in a way that would allow me to share it with others. I decided that my knowing would be indisputably true if it worked for others as it did for me. If not, I was just lucky and had a beautiful dream, nothing more and nothing less.

Since then, I have devoted all my time and efforts to sharing my experience with others around the world. My test is not over yet, and I cannot say how my life-long endeavor will turn out eventually. However, if you are open to this possibility, and apply these concepts and principles to your life, I am certain, from my experience of witnessing hundreds of thousands of people making positive changes in their lives through LifeParticles, that at least your health in all aspects will improve remarkably.

THE UNIVERSAL LANGUAGE

How do ants and bats know beforehand that an earthquake is coming? How can a salmon find its way back home? How do migrating birds orient themselves in the wide blue yonder? The amazing abilities of various animals have been much talked about, but their exact mechanisms still remain, in large part, a mystery. Scientists suspect that animals are able to utilize their senses to detect subtle shifts in Earth's magnetic web. In fact, all life-forms, composed of the same ultimate stuff of reality despite their apparent differences, have the ability to detect minute changes in the vibration of that primordial "stuff."

It is likely that we humans have been dependent too long on navigating our way through life based on language and thought, and have lost the natural fine sense to detect and attune ourselves to the unity of Energy-Consciousness, LifeParticles. Therefore, in order to recognize the subtle vibration of Energy-Consciousness and comprehend its implications, we first need to reawaken our inherent sense of it—much like attaining a new way of communication or a new language, a new language of subtle vibration of energy and consciousness, or simply LifeParticles. However, unlike learning a skill, this does not require any tool or knowledge. Since you already possess this sense and more fundamentally, are made of LifeParticles, all you have to do is unblock the blocked parts and awaken the sleeping parts of your being to access it. Using the language of LifeParticles does not go contrary to the use of verbalized languages; actually, this new language supports and enriches our current language, allowing us to experience those aspects of life that otherwise would have been inaccessible.

This is the language of feeling, rather than understanding. To experiment with it, and begin to enliven and strengthen it, ask yourself, "How would I feel if . . ." and just feel. Feel how other people feel, how the oceans, forests, and animals feel, how the Earth feels.

The language of the unity of Energy-Consciousness, LifeParticles can be a universal language for all humans and for all life-forms because it is not culturally biased. It doesn't require knowledge and skills, but affects all life-forms and all beings, and represents reality on all levels of manifestation from Nothing to the observed universe. Through this new language, you can deliver your feeling and intent to others, and consciously experience your connection to all being.

In recent years there have been numerous reports of the kind of subtle, nonverbal communication I am referring to. One was a simple classroom experiment you can replicate yourself in your kitchen with a couple of cups half full of water and two onions. Place the onions on top of the cups so that they don't fall in completely, but with the bottoms of the onions into the water a little bit. Then set them beside the window where they can get a decent amount of sunlight. They will start to sprout and grow in a couple of days. There's nothing unusual about a living plant growing with an appropriate supply of water and sunlight. It is just normal.

However, if you give differentiated attention to the onions, they, in response to the kind of attention they receive, will begin to show growth in different ways. How to differentiate your attention? It's pretty simple. Whenever you see them, say "I love you" to one onion and "I hate you" to the other. To make it easier, you can write the sentences on sticky notes, place them on the cups, and read them aloud whenever you pass by. You will be surprised to see how differently the onions respond. One will sprout healthy, strong stems; the other, weak and distorted stems that will soon begin to wither. I saw teachers use this experiment to teach their students the importance of a positive attitude toward other people and all living things.

A similar and more scientifically debated example is the story of water, as studied in the laboratory of a Japanese doctor, Masaru Emoto. Can water think? Can it learn? After reading the book *Water Knows the Answers: The Hidden Messages in Water Crystals*, you may believe that water can reflect human emotions and has the power to listen and see.

In his experiments, Dr. Emoto refrigerated different kinds of natural water and photographed the droplets with a high-speed camera as they began to freeze, capturing images of beautiful crystals. After several trials, he came to realize that tap water crystals, contaminated with chlorine, are different from those of pure water from wells, glaciers, and springs. The pure water formed crystals that were beautifully patterned and symmetrical, but the tap water crystals were incoherent and disorganized, not beautiful at all.

Dr. Emoto wondered what would happen to the water if he exposed it to music. He was surprised to find that when a bottle of water was placed between two speakers playing classical music, such as Mozart's Symphony no. 40 in G Minor, beautiful and bright crystal hexagons were formed. But when exposed to heavy rock music with angry lyrics and curse words, the crystals shattered into small pieces.

Dr. Emoto continued his research by placing a label reading "Thank you" on some of the bottles and "You fool" on others, and left them overnight. Later he froze the water samples and took photos of the crystals. He found that the water crystals were different depending on the words. The water reacted to affectionate words like *thank you*, and *love* by forming crystals in the shape of a smiling flower, but created crystals with unbalanced and distorted structure in response to curses like *damn it* and *fool*.

Currently, there is no science that can explain this. Indeed, it seems that the scientific community doesn't care much about it. We don't know exactly how the onions or water respond to the messages they receive. Interestingly, the experiments come up with the same results whether the messages are written, spoken, or communicated in different languages. This would indicate that the objects, such as onions or water, respond not to the specific words or sentences but to the meaning or intention of the speaker, or the quality of attention behind the words. Dr. Emoto pointed out that "everything in the world exists through a kind of vibration, and everything that vibrates in the world influences something else." Again, what we see here is energy and consciousness. A person's attention, which is basically concentrated consciousness, creates the differences.

I, like you, don't believe onions are particularly smarter than other plants or vegetables. We will see the same results if we repeat the onion experiments using carrots or potatoes. Also, several observations of the capability of plants to be aware of the conditions of other life-forms, such as joy or pain, have been reported.

Water may have an affinity for us because our body is 70 to 80 percent water throughout our lifetime. But the ingredients of water are among the most common elements here on Earth and in the universe. If water responds to our mind, why shouldn't air or even empty space do the same? We just don't know yet how to photograph it like the crystallized water droplets.

If, according to quantum physics, our attention can create changes in the state of small things such as subatomic particles, and this applies to bigger objects as well, should we be surprised to find that onions, carrots, potatoes, and water droplets respond to our attention? We can communicate thoughts and intentions, and create changes in the world through Energy-Consciousness, the universal medium of LifeParticles. This understanding prompts us to rethink and expand our understanding about our communications and relationships with other people—indeed, with all things—and also about the primary tool we currently use for such communications and relationships; that is, our language.

SOME THINGS CANNOT BE EXPRESSED IN WORDS

In our everyday life, we often come up against the limitations of language when we seek to express certain subtle sensations or resonances that we feel deep inside. Have you ever had the experience of feeling frustrated because you could not put into words that deepest something within your heart? Or have you had a sudden unexpected glimpse of the truth of reality, 95 percent of which is not observed and therefore indescribable by our current language? Not only in creative areas of human activity, but also in activities characterized by reason and intellect like science and mathematics, many of the most profound discoveries were reported to have come through intuition rather than sequential analysis processed by linguistic understanding.

The truth was seen or felt first, and then it managed to find expression in language to be communicated to others.

Many spiritual traditions have understood the limitation of filtering perception through the framework of language. Zen, for example, is a practice that aspires to see things directly, without naming or thinking. By shutting down the thinker and quieting the chatter inside, we can see the deeper layers of being, and come closer to truth.

In the great spiritual traditions, great teachings were often delivered without words by a simple action, like holding up a flower as Sakyamuni Buddha did about 2,500 years ago, or with a gentle, hardly noticeable smile, or just by keeping quiet and not saying anything. And then, of course, people started to analyze and interpret the gestures and expressions: the smile must mean this, the flower symbolizes something else . . . and so on. The interpretations are recorded into a book and that book eventually becomes the sacred text of the particular tradition. Once they attain the status of a sacred text, the interpreted words gain and exercise an authority that controls and limits the behavior of the people. People start to memorize, chant, and imitate the words of the sacred book.

That's how the living Truth of life and enlightenment becomes mummified, leaving only dried-out forms and structures without the rich flavor and fragrance of its real content, whose essence is in *being* it, not talking about it.

Truth is truth, not the explanations of Truth. Truth is a living, moving process. Truth is constantly undulating and vibrating. You can become one with the Truth, but you cannot adequately explain it. This is what happens: In the *experience* of

Truth, subject and object merge in a oneness of pure knowing. This is pure, nondual, awakened awareness. Then, in the *recognition* of Truth, I realize I have seen and I know the Truth. Finally, in the *explanation* of Truth, I begin to use words to say what it means.

In order to recognize the Truth, you have to separate yourself from the Truth; and to explain the Truth, you have to separate yourself from the recognition. This is why a wordsmithed Truth is nothing but a shadow of the shadow of the Truth. If Buddha had yawned instead of holding up a flower, would that gesture have been any less representative of the Truth?

On the other hand, it is sometimes possible to represent the Truth with words. However, in that case, it is not the words themselves but the power of the vibration of the words as spoken by the speaker, and the lively responsiveness of the surrounding atmosphere, that conspire to make the speech into an experience or an event that allows you a glimpse into the Truth. There is a world of difference between being at an event and reading about it in a newspaper article. If you try to approach the Truth only through words, this is akin to reading the transcript of the talk later on. Such is the limitation of language. Although it will do for our everyday lives, language is too small a vessel to hold the water of the Truth and too rough a mesh to catch the flow of the Truth.

UNFILLABLE HOLES

When we come across new experiences, we want to understand them, and understanding an experience is essentially the same as organizing it into words. When you say things like, "I don't understand what I went through . . ." or "I just have no idea . . ." you actually mean that you cannot find the words to describe your experiences. And as our society becomes increasingly complicated and intricate, our experiences become more difficult to put into words.

In an ever-continuing effort to codify these experiences we are constantly inventing more words and continuously advancing the technology of information processing to dizzying heights. Today, we have managed to quantify any and every word into binary bits that can be expressed in 0s and 1s. In this fashion, words can become digitized signals and thereby can be managed and processed by machines and computers. Not only words, but also light and sound can also be transmitted in bits. MP3 players and digital cameras are examples of such technology. This advance, often called the Digital Revolution, is designed to make all our experiences describable with combinations of the simple signals, 0 and 1. But if verbal language is a step removed from the reality it is trying to describe, isn't digital language yet another step further away?

Take a digital camera and snap a picture of the most beautiful flower you have ever seen, its delicate petals shining with fresh dew. Now download this image into your computer and zoom in. As you magnify the image, soon you will no longer see a flower, dew, or anything you can recognize. All you will see are dots of varying colors, and spaces in between those dots. Then, you will no longer even see the colors of the dots. They will just be jagged-edged blobs. So what happened to the flower, its petals trembling in the early morning chill, sunlight bouncing off the dewdrops and creating the tiniest images of the perfect rainbow? The lively vibration of life that you felt when looking at the flower escaped through the holes in the digitized images. Truth, and life, cannot be captured by language in any form except for the universal, nonverbal language of LifeParticles, the particles of Nothing, which are the life energy itself that connects not only all beings in the universe, but also bridges existence and nonexistence. These are particles of the unity of Energy-Consciousness. This is the stuff that can fill any gap in our experience and perception, and it is the medium that can be used in our communication with all people, all life-forms, and all beings.

THE WORLD DESCRIBED BY
THE NEW LANGUAGE OF LIFEPARTICLES

LifeParticles, the ultimate substance of Energy-Consciousness, is what we really are. It is the ultimate commonality that encompasses and connects not only you and me, but also all beings and the entire universe. Through the awareness of LifeParticles, you can consciously experience your connection to all others, and communicate with them beyond languages.

When we look at ourselves and the world from the perspective of LifeParticles, we become able to understand some basic laws of nature.

Everything Is Connected

All beings, including myself, are made up of the same substance, LifeParticles. All beings, including myself, ceaselessly interact and communicate with each other through an exchange of LifeParticles. Despite the apparent differences and functional separations, ultimate commonality connects all beings on a deeper level of reality. Through this connection, all beings affect each other. Through this connection, all beings reflect each other. Whatever we do, we do it to ourselves. Whatever comes out of us comes back to us.

I Create My Reality

LifeParticles and everything made up of LifeParticles vibrate with infinite potential. These potentials manifest in response to my intentions and choices to become realities. Through observation, I create reality. I am a creative observer. As a creative observer, I create my experiences of life, good or bad. The life that I am experiencing, good or bad, is the collective result of the choices that I have made, knowingly or unknowingly. By denying this, I deny myself the power to change my reality. By acknowledging and accepting this, I acknowledge that I have the power to create my destiny.

I Am Unlimited and Timeless

In essence, LifeParticles are neither created nor destroyed. Therefore, at the level of LifeParticles, neither are we. The flow of LifeParticles, or the unity of Energy-Consciousness, causes the phenomenon of life. When the flow takes a visible form, we call it birth. When the form resolves into an invisible substance, we call it death. What we call My Life is a phenomenon that spans these two points, but life itself is not limited to the space between. It is a continuous flow of LifeParticles, manifesting itself in countless forms. As a phenomenon, my life—or any life—has a beginning and ending, but life itself doesn't. Then, which one is truly me, a phenomenon that lasts only between these two points called birth and death, or life itself that underlies all these phenomena, creating all the changes while itself remaining unchanged?

I Live for the Good of All

Ask yourself this: If the author is correct that we are all connected, and are the manifestation of the same ultimate commonality, then how would I treat other people, other life-forms, and all other beings? By using the power of LifeParticles, we can create our reality. Then, what reality would you like to create? What kind of world would you like to see?

By acknowledging and accepting the ultimate commonality, we can naturally and voluntarily develop the attitude of compassion and benevolence toward other people, other life-forms, and all beings. We will want to live for the good of all because we know that's the way we benefit ourselves, too. At least we will refrain from harming others intentionally. Developing this attitude toward others will eventually make our world more tolerant, peaceful, and harmonious.

This is the foundation of all the changes we are going to

make. You don't need to be a believer. An experimental trial or even skepticism is okay. Just allow yourself to take on this new perspective and act as if you are LifeParticles. Test the idea, apply its principles, and see how it works.

CHAPTER FOUR

The True Power to Change the World

EXPERIENCING NOTHING

In the tradition of Tao, enlightenment means attaining the status of selflessness. In Korean, it is called *Mu-Ah*. *Mu* means "No," or "Nothing," and *Ah* means "Me," or "Self." Combined, it means no-me-ness, or selflessness, which becomes possible when you recognize yourself as Nothing. How will this happen, or how can we experience this?

Experience of Nothing is much closer than you think. For example, if you close your eyes and begin to feel your breath, it will instantly become deeper and slower, and your mind will become calmer. Then gradually you'll become aware of your body, or more precisely the subtle sense of energy inside and around your body. At that moment, you exist as Energy-Consciousness, not as names, jobs, duties, roles, desires, and so on.

You can perceive it with your eyes open, too. Look around you. You will see many objects, from the clock on the wall to the cup on the table. Without any conscious thought, observe these objects silently. How do you know they are actually there? When we look at things, we just focus on them and don't usually pay attention to what is behind and around them. However, nothing exists alone; everything exists in relation to others. We recognize objects and individuals through the contrast between them and the background behind them. This applies to the experience of hearing sound, too. When we listen to music, we recognize the melody and rhythm not just because of the sound itself, but also because of the silence between the notes, or more precisely through the contrast between the sound and the silence.

I see the clock on the wall. Actually it doesn't matter whether it is a clock, mirror, picture frame, or whatever. These are all secondary perceptions—the primary perception is that there is *something*. Before I recognize the specific names and uses of these things, I know there's something, and I know it through the contrast between these things and the background. If we extend this a little further, how do we know that there's anything at all? Because of the background. And what is the ultimate background of anything that exists? It is Nothingness and Emptiness. Zero. It is the purest mind, the perceived Nothingness.

Many people may feel that this still sounds abstract, and may want more tangible experience of the pure mind, Zero, and Nothing. So, let's move on and take another step into Nothing, for a more direct and personal experience of it.

THE ENLIGHTENMENT THAT WE NEED

If I say that you are already enlightened, would you believe that?

We entertain many interesting ideas about things, even when we really don't know about them. Enlightenment, God, heaven, and death, to mention a few, are good examples.

What is enlightenment? Realizing Nothing and recovering Zero have been called enlightenment in many spiritual traditions. In the Korean tradition of Tao, as mentioned earlier, enlightenment is known as *Mu-Ah. Mu* means "No," or "Nothing," and *Ah* means "Me." So it is no-me-ness, or egoless-ness. It doesn't mean disappearance of you as a person. Instead, it means realizing the true, unchanging nature of the person you happen to be.

Many people, through diverse spiritual practices and disciplines have sought enlightenment. Various phenomena, some of them potentially quite captivating, may occur along the path of spiritual development whether it leads to true enlightenment or not. They can be helpful if used wisely, but are neither the sign of enlightenment nor the requirements for enlightenment. These can include extrasensory perception (sometimes called ESP), remote viewing, or "miraculous" healing. However, the essence of enlightenment, above and beyond all phenomena, is a *big* understanding, which gives you a deep and wide perspective to see the world as a whole, and a capacity to accept with compassion all that is.

Within this big understanding, we realize that we are eternal life, which exists alone and on its own: that distinctions such as good or evil, like or dislike, blessing or curse, and birth or death don't exist on that level of reality. We realize that we already have—we already *are*—everything we need for enlightenment. If you can acknowledge and accept this, it is enlightenment. You will discover that you have unshakeable, absolute truthfulness inside that urges you to make right choices for the benefit of all, beyond your egoistic desires and interests. When this expanded, beautiful state of life becomes your daily living reality, enlightenment is complete.

Basically it is your choice. No matter what spiritual path you have taken, no matter what experiences you have had, choice is still choice. Spiritual development doesn't happen automatically. It is choosing the eye of Tao that sees both the whole view of things from a distance and the core of reality from deep inside. This is what I mean by a big understanding.

The choice is to live a spiritual life; to live a bigger life; to live a life of service to Earth and the whole; it's choosing every day and every hour to live by your true nature at all levels of being rather than live as an individual person only on the material dimension of being.

We can test this only by taking action. The ancient teaching of Tao tells us that knowing what you really are is wisdom, and living it is virtue. This may sound like a challenge, but it isn't. Can there be any easier way of life than living by your true nature, living as what you really are?

ALREADY ENLIGHTENED AND DIVINE

Back to the question that I asked you earlier: If I say that you are already enlightened, would you believe that? Do you want me to prove it?

I assume your answer is yes. Okay. We'll need only a simple exercise for this. While sitting down, please wrap your arms around your knees. Lean your body to one side. Try to take your feet off the ground. But be careful not to lean too far: falling over is not part of this exercise! While holding the position, please answer this question:

Is your body slanted?

I assume your answer is yes. How do you know that your body is slanted? If you think it is because you can see that your body is slanted, then try again with your eyes closed. You will still feel the awkward balance, and you will know that you are leaning to the side. How do you know? Because of your inner sense of balance.

It's true. As you learned in high school biology, your sense of balance is located in your inner ear. It is not easy to describe its shape here, but you can think of it as a closed tube that has liquid in it, like a level, or balance measurer, used in construction. When your body is slanted, this tube is also slanted, but the liquid in it, as liquid does, maintains its horizontal position. This means one end of the tube has more liquid than the other end. Sensors on each end feel the change of pressure and send the signal to your brain. This is how the sense of balance works and how you know you are slanted.

The main point I am making is that you know you are

slanted because there is something inside you that is not.

Where am I going with this? Here's another example that will make it clear. When you are not being truthful, you know it. How do you know? Bingo! Because, deep down, you are truthful. No matter what you do, think, or say, there is absolute truthfulness inside you that is not affected by what you think, say, or do. This absolute truthfulness reflects exactly what you do like a mirror. It is a perfect scale inside us, a scale that weighs truthfulness like the sense of balance that tells you whether you are balanced or not. Even if you try to ignore it, deny it, hide from it, or run away from it, you will feel it when you are not being true, because of the absolute truthfulness deep within.

This absolute truthfulness is not your achievement. If we had to achieve absolute truthfulness by our own efforts, humanity would be hopeless. Just recall how many times you have not been perfectly truthful today so far. What about yesterday? How many lies has each of us told in a year or in our lifetime? Even with one small grain of untruthfulness—a slight exaggeration, an uncomfortable detail left out—it is already over. That's because 99.9999... percent is not 100 percent. Then how could we achieve absolute truthfulness by our own effort?

But here is the important thing: No matter how untrue we may have been outwardly, there was always truthfulness inside us. We didn't create it. This truthfulness has been there all the time. It was given from the very beginning. It is absolute and unconditional, attributes that we believe to be divine. The absolute truthfulness inside comes from our divine nature: One, Tao, Nothing, Hananim, Zero. Can anything be purer than Zero? Can anything be more true than Nothing? Nothing and

Zero, because of their pure, undivided, untarnished nature, can reflect and weigh everything exactly the way it is, absolutely truthfully. Nothing, Zero, the ultimate reality, is the foundation of the absolute truthfulness, the perfect scale inside us. It is inside us because that is what we are made of: One, Nothing, Energy-Consciousness, LifeParticles.

That absolute, ultimate reality is always there within us (as it is everywhere else, as well). Whether we are aware of it or not, it is there, like the sun shining behind the clouds, invisible because of the clouds, but undeniably there. The sun of our inner nature, the LifeParticle Sun, is always shining, whether we see it or not. And because it is already there, we don't need to create or achieve it. We just have to acknowledge it. Acknowledging that you are nothing other than the divine nature and not separate from it is your choice. This is what I meant when I said that "I got enlightened to the fact that there's nothing to get enlightened to" in response to a questioner who asked what I got enlightened to. It is not achieving something. It is acknowledging what's already there. Therefore, enlightenment is choice.

No matter what stage we are at in our spiritual journey, whether we are beginners or have been traveling a spiritual path for years or decades; and no matter how awakened or asleep we are, there is always absolute truthfulness—the oneness and nothingness—which is our true nature. Our true nature doesn't need any explanation or demonstration to know itself. It just *knows* because knowing is part of its nature. This true nature resides in everyone. This is the meaning of the statement that everyone is already enlightened.

However, our mind, with the capability to focus, think,

understand, and know, views the separate individual self, or ego, as something real because for so many years that's all it has witnessed and experienced. Even if a person has a glimpse of the Truth, as I believe most people do—a taste of the inner silence, expansiveness, and joy of their true self—and even if they recognize that it is real and is their true nature, they are still under the sway of the ego.

But because they now know what their true nature is, they see what's missing in their lives. What is missing is integrity in its deepest sense: their life doesn't completely manifest their true nature. Life without integrity doesn't feel good; it feels empty and meaningless. From this point, their life purpose is to close the gap. This is the beginning of devoted practice, or *Su-Haeng* in Korean. Nobody is asking or forcing them to do so. They do this because they truly want it. The goal they aspire to is completion, the only thing they want in their lives.

For some people, acknowledging and accepting the Truth and becoming one with the Truth can happen simultaneously. It may happen like a quiet dawning. For others, it may come like lightning and thunder. There are innumerable ways for it to happen. Awakening to the Truth is an individual process that can happen instantaneously, or over time.

When this absolute truthfulness is perceived, we recognize and experience it as conscience, and this is what I meant at the beginning of this chapter by personal and direct experience of Nothing, or the absolute truthfulness. Nothing, or absolute truthfulness, may sound remote to many people, but conscience is what they have known throughout their lives whether they are good friends with it or not. Conscience is the perceived absolute truthfulness. Reviving our never-lost connection to conscience—listening for it, opening to its messages for us—is another way we can recalibrate our lives, attuning to the Zero within.

THE POWER OF CONSCIENCE

Conscience is one of the mysteries of human behavior. It has been one of the most debated subjects in psychology, in philosophy, and even in economics. Conscience can hardly be explained by selfishness or egotism, which are claimed to be the most basic traits of an individual human being. On the contrary: conscience is unreasonable or irrational when seen from the perspective of egotistic motivation. What is perhaps most surprising about conscience is that everybody has it. We may have taken it so for granted that we rarely wonder what it is, why we have it, or how it works; but the fact that everybody has conscience, regardless of personalities, living conditions, or backgrounds, is worth deep contemplation.

Why do some people choose to be truthful even when doing so is expected to bring loss or personal disadvantage? Why is it uncomfortable or even painful for us not to follow the call of conscience? It's because conscience is the manifestation of our divine nature, the absolute truthfulness that we all have inside, that resides beyond the instinctive desire to survive. Because it is our nature, we don't recognize it all the time, just as you don't need to be conscious of your humanity to be human, of masculinity to be male, or of femininity to be female. You just are.

We become aware of our nature only when it is doubted or challenged. Please tell me, when were you most sharply aware of your conscience? Was it when you were following it, or when you were betraying it? It is paradoxical, but at the very moment when we refuse to follow our conscience and refuse to be truthful, we become all the more aware of the presence of conscience and the absolute truthfulness inside. Because it is based on our nature, we feel comfortable when we follow our conscience, so comfortable that we don't usually notice we are following it. When we don't follow it, we feel unnatural, uncomfortable, unhappy, and even pained, and become sharply aware that we are denying or going against our conscience.

A quiet little voice of warning, or a feeling of roughness in the heart when we are about to say, do, or even just think something hurtful—those are a divine call to keep us on the right track. And so are the feelings of regret if we've ignored that warning and gone ahead with what we knew wasn't right. On the other hand, following our conscience is its own reward, as the Belgian Nobel Prize–winning poet, Maurice Maeterlinck, observed: "An act of goodness is of itself an act of happiness," he said. "No reward coming after the event can compare with the sweet reward that went with it." You may ignore the call of your conscience, but you can't deny its presence; it is rooted in your very nature.

Conscience is different from morality, norms, or ethics. Morality or ethics are relative, and depend on the social, cultural, and historical context. What is viewed to be moral in one culture can be disdained as immoral in another. An action that is lauded as heroic in one context can be condemned as an unforgivable crime or sin in a different context. However, conscience is not determined by the context. It is the will to truthfulness, performing right action, no matter what.

Because of the presence of conscience, each and every one of us has the potential for greatness. Because of the undeniable presence of conscience, we can choose to be truthful even when the choice means personal loss. We can choose to undertake a great action—unselfish, courageous, daringly creative—that looks unreasonable and irrational to the eye of Ego.

A few years ago, when there was a risk of nuclear reactor meltdown at Fukushima in Japan after a massive tsunami, the local government asked for volunteers who would work near the reactor to recover the power line to supply the cooling water. About 120 people came. They were volunteers, not government officials or hired technicians. They consisted of diverse age groups and backgrounds. Some were young but others were over 60. Some people came from town, others flew from distant cities.

Working near a nuclear reactor, which has the risk of melting down any moment, is not something that people normally think they can do, even if a large reward is offered. But something inside them that cares for the safety of all more than their personal safety, woke up and motivated them to take action. That was how they came. That shows what a different person we can be when the absolute truthfulness wakes up, and when we begin to follow its call.

Because everybody has conscience, whether or not we can be great beings is not determined merely by its presence inside us. Instead, it is determined by the choice to acknowledge its presence and follow its lead. Absolute truthfulness, and conscience as its manifestation, are within everybody. Acknowledging it is wisdom, and living it is virtue.

THE CHALLENGES TO CONSCIENCE

Recognizing conscience is one thing. Following it is another. For some people, it is just a little more difficult to follow, for several reasons.

Sick, afraid, despondent . . . , do these descriptions sound remote or familiar? It seems like these are becoming a general description of the human condition all over the world. Look around. How are the people around you? How about yourself? How many people do you see in your daily life who don't belong to any or all of these categories?

These are the conditions that make it hard to follow conscience. When people are sick, afraid, and despondent, their will is weak and easily broken, and their mind readily manipulated. With a small threat or temptation, their mind changes.

These conditions are closely related. First of all, for many people, their biggest concern is their health. Being unsure of their ability to take care of their health deeply shadows their outlook on life, their attitude, and confidence. And it must be said that the current health care system has made a big contribution to this state of affairs. It is generally agreed that prevention produces far better results, with much less cost, as compared with intervention. Or simply put, health is easier to maintain when we are healthy, than to restore when we become ill. It's common sense.

The current health care system works the other way. Its primary focus is on intervention, not on prevention. I have read that the majority of the cost of intervention is not for a cure but a diagnosis, and this does not surprise me because expensive, high-tech, high-energy equipment is being used for diagnosis, even when it is not really needed. To our frustration and bewilderment, in many cases the result of such diagnostic procedures is that they cannot find exactly what's wrong. Spending so much money, time, and energy just to find out that we don't know exactly what's wrong . . . that's an embarrassing paradox.

The more tragic side effect of this system is the general belief that taking care of health requires highly specialized expertise and we, the nonexperts, cannot take care of our own health. A related belief is that health is something special that you need to make enormous effort to achieve. We came to have this belief because we have become so accustomed to living in sickness. But look around at other things in nature. What kind of medications do the wildflowers and trees take, and what doctors do the wild animals go to see? Our belief that health is something that we need to achieve by effort is the first thing that we need to change in our perspective on health. Health, instead of being something to be acquired with effort and cost, is and should be the most natural state of life.

Financial insecurity accentuates the feeling of fear and crisis. The vast majority of people, even those who are quite well-off, feel that their financial future is insecure. Most are in debt, which is usually increasing rather than decreasing. Insecurity about finances, added to uncertainty about health, makes many people afraid.

What makes the picture darker is the mood of despondency that underlies our mentality and behavior. Are *you* hopeful? Seriously?

The mood of "doom and gloom" is not new. Stories about the good old days, based on the perception or assumption that the world is getting worse, have existed throughout human history. We can find similar stories in any culture, either now or then. Even when we passionately speak of positive possibilities for the future, we often find ourselves saying so without really believing our own words. Just think how many times you've said something positive without truly believing in it:

"Don't worry, I'm sure it will work out."

"You'll feel better tomorrow."

Because this mood of resignation and lack of hope is so prevalent, it's worth considering where it comes from. Is it grounded in reality? Or are we sick in mind?

We know how subjective our view of the world is. Depending on our thoughts, emotions, and current circumstances, our view of life and the world changes easily. This means it is reasonable to search for the factor or factors inside us that affect or determine our mentality and are conducive to the sense of despondency. Of course, the world may actually be doomed, and our dark and gloomy mood may have legitimate causes. But searching for external factors is not very productive because world events are generally not under our direct control and take time to redirect and change. So what do you think is the primary factor inside you that affects your not-so-bright view of the world and life?

Maybe I can be a little more straightforward. Do you believe in yourself? If you don't believe in yourself, it will be hard or almost impossible to have a positive belief in the world and life. How can a person genuinely believe in the positive transformation of the world if he/she doesn't believe that he/she can be a better person? Then how can we believe in ourselves? Is this a matter of therapy or self-hypnosis? I don't think repeating passionately that you believe in yourself before a mirror will work for you. That's because of our conscience—the absolute truthfulness that watches us with serene, ocean-blue eyes! We can make believe to others, but not to ourselves.

My answer is this: wake up. Accept and acknowledge what you really are. Realize your true value, the absolute value. And more importantly, *live it!* Do it! Because if you say one thing, and do something different, how can your conscience trust you? Self-trust comes from integrity. Where else can it come from?

I guess I need to be careful of the tone of my voice here because the word integrity in many people's minds is closely associated with promises they made and did not fulfill, and it thereby makes them get defensive and feel guilty. The idea that I have about integrity is that we can practice it in the same way that we exercise to build muscles. To build muscles, we try to lift heavy things. Sometimes we succeed, other times we don't. However, we build muscles not only when we succeed. Actually we build more muscles when we fail because we have used all the more effort to lift the weights. The important thing is trying it anyway, doing it anyway. You don't need to do it all at once, but do it, even a small part of it, truthfully. When you succeed, celebrate. When you don't, acknowledge it, and learn from the experience. You will build the muscle of integrity anyway. (I will explain how to build this muscle in chapter six when I explain how to develop the potential of our brain.)

With the muscles of our body, we can lift and move heavy things. With the muscle of integrity, we can turn intention into powerful action. That's how we can earn trust from our conscience, and can truly believe in ourselves. When we truly believe in ourselves, it will be much easier to believe in the world and life, too.

WHERE IS THE HOPE?

At this time in history, sick, afraid, and despondent are the general conditions that affect the majority of people almost everywhere. It's difficult and challenging to follow the call of conscience when we're under the dark veil of these forces. At the same time, it's painful not to follow it.

When you become healthy, courageous, and hopeful, following your conscience becomes much easier. When people are healthy, courageous, and hopeful, it's difficult to bend their mind and will. You can't force them to do what you'd like them to do against their will. They will speak out what they believe, and stand up and do what is right even when it means a loss to them.

I am hopeful because I have witnessed this change throughout my life. From the realization of what I really am, I became hopeful, courageous, and passionate for life, and I felt responsible for the general condition of humanity and the Earth because they are not separate from me. I started sharing my realization and LifeParticles at a small public park in Korea.

One person, paralyzed in half of his body by a stroke, was my first student. I started to exercise with him. The exercise wasn't a systemized set of body movements. I just allowed my body to do whatever felt right, and asked him to follow. It worked and the person was healed. Seeing what happened, more people came and that's how this movement grew. What I witnessed in all of these people was the change from sick, afraid, and despondent to healthy, courageous, and hopeful.

The most amazing thing was that most of them ended up following the path that I took: They wanted to share with other people the good they experienced. They went to the park as I did before. Soon the number of the parks where these people taught exercise grew to more than 3,000. It is now one of the biggest spontaneous cultural movements in Korea, and it is expanding to other areas of community life such as homes, schools, workplaces, community centers, and local governments.

THE TRUE MIRACLE

They all started from their need for and interest in health. Not a few people experienced recovery from "incurable" diseases. But those are not true miracles. The true miracle is the recovery of the power of conscience. When they became healthy, courageous, and hopeful, they began to use the power of their conscience.

When the power of conscience is recovered, the most noticeable and meaningful change in people's perception or behavior is their willingness to put the benefit of all before their personal benefit, to find their true purpose in life in benefiting all. This is a big change for those who have lived their lives solely or primarily for their own benefit. Because conscience, the divine nature within us, sees everything as connected, what's good for all is always its priority. If we see things with a long view, this is actually a wise choice, because what's good for you but not good for all won't be good for you either, eventually. This spirit, this willingness to benefit all is called *Hong-Ik* in Korean. This is the essential teaching of the Scripture of Heavenly Code, as explained in chapter two, which teaches us that One, or Nothing, is the ultimate reality, and that we humans have heaven and earth as one within us.

I believe that this great mind, the spirit of Hong-Ik, the eternal wholeness of the universe, is inside everyone. When this mind is awakened, everyone will know that we are not separate and will naturally develop the desire to benefit each other. I also believe this awakening will help people to resolve their personal problems and help all of us to resolve global issues and challenges. We already have the technology, information, and resources that we need. The key to resolving our current global crisis is the mind that cares about the Earth and loves all lives as one's own, rather than any systems or technologies. As the Bible says, "Love thy neighbor as thyself." This is the sole drive that moves me to write this and talk about LifeParticles as a new way of seeing ourselves and reality.

The title of this chapter is "The True Power to Change the World." What do you think is the true power? Does it come from Wall Street? The White House? You have seen world events unfold, witnessed the behavior of leaders in business, government, religion, health care. Does it seem to you that the absolute truth within is the final compass that they rely on to make a decision, and the benefit of all is the goal for their decision?

Conscience is the true power. It resides within us. The intention to be absolutely truthful and the willingness to put the benefit of all before personal benefit hold the power to change the world. This intention and willingness is of course ethical choice, but it is also the most natural, reasonable, and intelligent choice when we realize what we really are. If people begin to use the full power of conscience in all the choices they make in their everyday life, from presidential elections to purchasing things in the grocery store, the world will change.

Because I know that we all have this mind, I am hopeful. We just need to begin to use its power. You will be amazed by the changes you can create.

If somebody asks me what enlightenment is, I say that it is simply recovering conscience. If someone else asks why we need to meditate, I say, "It is to find and awaken conscience, the spirit of Hong-Ik, inside your heart."

CHAPTER FIVE

The Absolute Scale

CONSCIENCE ON A SOCIAL PLANE

Conscience is the absolute truthfulness perceived, which comes from Nothing, our true nature, and as such reflects things exactly the way they are. How can we apply this to the choices and judgments that we make in our daily lives? Furthermore, how can we apply the idea of absolute truthfulness on a social level?

We started this conversation with the shared perception that we need to change. Now we need to take a closer look at what exactly it is that we want to change.

There are, of course, many possibilities, but I propose to consider something fundamental. Rather than the kind of change that simply takes what we already have and augments it, like adding more power to our cars or more speed to our computers, I believe the kind of change we need now is a change of direction. And we need that change not because we are unsure of where we're heading. We know very well where we're heading, we know where we'll end up if we keep to our current direction, and we are deeply aware that it's not the right destination—not where we want to find ourselves. So a change of direction is imperative.

Making changes requires making new and different choices, choices that are more conscious, more enlightened, and more life-supporting. Continuing to do what we have been doing so far is also a choice, but not one that will bring any meaningful improvement. I would suggest that before we can intelligently make new choices, a thorough reevaluation is in order. We need to look carefully at what we value, what we have, and what we desire to make sure these are really important to us and represent what we truly want.

The factors we have to reevaluate are not new. Rather, they are values and standards we have taken for granted for a long time, such as success as a personal goal of life and competition as a way to achieve that goal; gaining a dominant position in the market as a company goal and productivity and profit as the way to achieve it; increase of GDP as an indicator of a strong national economy; wielding dominant military power to maintain peace; health as a state that requires great cost and help from experts. . . .

Are these assumptions really valid? For most of us, these are ideas and values we just accepted as a matter of fact. We rarely question the validity of these commonly held beliefs. But that's exactly what we need to do now: examine values, principles, and assumptions that we have taken for granted. We're about to apply questions such as "Is this really important?" and "Is this what I truly want?" to ideas we have accepted uncritically and to behaviors we have been doing habitually.

Where do we begin this process of reevaluation of values? It makes sense to begin with our mind, which is the tool we use to evaluate. Once we make sure it is functioning as it should, we can feel confident in using it to think about our beliefs and priorities.

We use our minds in a way similar to how we use a scale. When we weigh something on a scale, that weight tells us what it's worth, what its value is. But what if your scale has not been accurately calibrated to zero, or what if somehow you had placed something else on the scale and forgotten to remove it? Then the reading, even with a perfect scale, cannot start at zero, and you cannot give a correct evaluation to anything that you weigh.

Each of us has a different weight already on his or her scale. Because of this, when we place any object on the scale, the reading will be off the mark by the weight of the objects already on the scale. We just don't remember or recognize that we have placed this burden upon our scale.

The weight, of course, consists of our beliefs, our past history, our values, all the mental and emotional baggage that we carry around that prevents us from seeing in a clear, unbiased, objective manner. It's akin to wearing a pair of color-tinted glasses but not knowing that you have them on.

We need to recalibrate our scale and remove our colored lenses, so we can start from the zero-point. This reminds me of using a calculator to make a series of calculations. When calculating multiple sets of numbers, you have to clear the previous calculation before you start a new one. And that is what we want: a fresh start.

RECALIBRATION

How can we restore the zero reading? What actually do we mean by restoring the zero reading? First of all, on a personal level, recalibration means clearing our perception and recovering our capacity for pure observation. This begins with becoming aware of our perception. Most of the time, when we are looking at something (or listening, tasting, etc.), we are not aware of who is perceiving—all our attention is on the object. Even less are we cognizant of the fact that we are looking through a specific mental-emotional frame or filter created by our past experiences, our hopes and expectations, our beliefs, and so on.

What color lenses do your glasses have? Is it possible to see the world with complete objectivity?

One way to approach more truthful perception is to see things from the perspective of the whole, which was described as the eye of Tao in the first chapter. It comes from realizing what we really are, beyond our names, beliefs, roles, job, education, race, nationality, religion, and all the other information that has been added on to our true nature. This doesn't mean we have to try to remove all this information and become a blank slate. We won't become blank minded even if we want to; the information will remain. However, if we acknowledge and accept what we really are, we will at least have a clear distinction between our true nature and our functional roles, between reality and phenomena, and between what is permanent and what is not, between what serves our nature and what serves our ego. After we become clear about this, we may still choose to keep things as they have been, retaining our name, job, nationality, and so on; but even when we do so, our purposes, mindsets, attitudes and behaviors, based on true self-knowledge, will be different. And the results will be different accordingly.

Recalibration comes from experiencing Nothingness, opening our awareness to emptiness as the ultimate reality and our essential nature. It is the purest mind, the Energy-Consciousness itself.

However, this is not the end. Actually, it is the beginning of the whole process of recalibration. Acknowledging and accepting what we really are is important because it allows us an open mind and fresh eyes to see things in a new, more balanced perspective.

The most important part of this process is applying the idea of recalibration to the measures we use to weigh the values that we strive for in our lives.

WHY POUNDS AND KILOGRAMS ARE IMPORTANT?

I travel quite a bit, partly because I love new experiences, but mostly because I go anywhere I can meet with people and share what I have realized about myself and about life.

As you know, jet lag is a challenge for a traveler. But thanks to my practice of energy and meditation, I can manage the challenge of jet lag quite easily. A bigger challenge for me are units and measurements such as currency, pounds, kilograms, ja, chi, ounce, meters, feet, yards, kilometers, miles, and so on. Because many countries I visit have different systems of units and measurements, to get a sense of what something feels like or looks like, I have to convert these units and measurements into those that are familiar to me.

Historically this was a challenge to the kings who unified different territories and domains, incorporating them into a larger nation. What the wise kings did after conquering a new territory was to decree that only one system of measurements be used in all transactions. That is, you could only use pounds and feet, when before you used grams and meters. Why was this important? When forcibly joining together two previously separate countries into one nation, it is important to plant the idea of a common nation and shared destiny among the people; otherwise, differences will eventually fester and rend the nation asunder.

More importantly, most conflicts between people arise not out of differences in culture or philosophy of life but out of unfair or unjust everyday transactions. This is more crucial in the case of a newly unified nation. Because a foundation of social trust has not been well established yet, you will need common, reliable standards of transaction more than ever. This is as true now as it was thousands of years ago. This is why wise kings of old, in order to establish a social order, made all units of measurement consistent. Fairness and trust in transaction begins with commonly accepted measurements. If every merchant had his own balances and weights, it would create chaos.

Even today, different parts of the world use different units of measurement and worth. The United States still insists on using miles and pounds while the rest of the world, with a few exceptions, uses the metric system. However, since conversion between the two systems of measurement is mathematically accurate, standardized, and universally accepted—and can be calculated in a few seconds by everyone—there is no cause for conflict any longer. The same goes for currency, with each country having its own system of money. Such differences in units of measurements are not really sources of conflict in the world.

What is a cause for conflicts and arguments is the different value that each person places upon the same item. Even if a McDonald's Quarter Pounder is a Quarter Pounder whether measured in kilograms or pounds, each person and each society confers different worth and meaning on the same hamburger. This is because people, cultures, and societies have different standards for measuring value. And until now, we considered such differences as a matter of fact, obvious and ubiquitous.

ABSOLUTE VS. RELATIVE VALUES AND LIMITS OF THE MARKET SYSTEM

The market has been the system of transaction through which different values came together and compromises were reached. A product's worth is decided by its demand and supply, dealt and transacted according to the value decreed on it by the market system. If a certain product is popular, its price goes up accordingly and more effort and money are invested into producing it. Such is the basic law of the market. However, we are stumped to explain certain phenomena that do not follow the supply and demand model and are coming to realize more and more the inherent limitations of the market system.

One of the underlying assumptions of the market system is that every player is informed fully and equally—provided with all relevant information that could have a bearing on a certain product or transaction. However, we know that such an assumption is unrealistic. Even worse, a fatal flaw in the market system is that life's most basic values are not "priceable," and therefore their real worth is not recognized and appreciated.

To make my point clearer and simpler, I would propose a distinction between absolute and relative values. By absolute values, I mean the values that are given by nature, such as air and water. Man-made values including cultures and social institutions are relative. Relative values are relative because their being valuable depends on social contexts and personal preferences and conditions of life.

One of the most dramatic examples is religion. One may argue that a religion is not a relative value because it deals with the Absolute. However, religion is not God himself or herself. It is a system of teaching *about* God. It is an explanation of God's way to human minds. But God, if he/she is truly God, doesn't need explanations to exist. Religion, especially, is a relative value in the sense that one religion is held as absolute truth by those who have faith in it; but to others, it can be viewed as a pagan practice or even a blasphemy.

The relative values are the values that you may like or dislike. However, the absolute values are not the things that you may like or dislike because your very existence absolutely needs them. Absolute values are the things that are important whether you like them or not. When you have lost some of the relative values, you may feel sad or uncomfortable, but loss of or disconnection from absolute values means termination of your life.

Although this is so obvious, what is happening today is that our current value system places relative values above absolute values. We are pursuing relative transient values at the cost of absolute lasting values. Our current market system is neither mature enough to deal with absolute values nor honest enough to acknowledge that such values exist—nor sophisticated enough to transact such values.

For example, if biodiversity is considered crucial to maintaining a stable ecosystem, what is the market value of a species? What about the market value of the clean environment that everyone agrees is essential to the survival of our human species? What is the value of salvation and immortality as promised in major religions? And how much would you pay for enlightenment?

Whether priceable or not through the market system, all these are transactions. Because we are all so intricately interconnected, our life is a series of transactions. Market transactions are just a miniscule part of the everyday information and energy exchange that we engage in ceaselessly. There are many methods of payment for these transactions. We can pay with money; we can pay with effort. A thoughtless action can become a lingering burden, and a kind smile can melt away the debt of several lifetimes.

The market system is a brilliant and potentially equitable system of determining the value of a product or a service. We have been using this system for a long time without questioning the assumptions behind it. Do they reflect our beliefs about what is important in life? And where do those beliefs come from? Are they conventional and socially conditioned? Or do they genuinely express our deepest concerns? Are they carefully considered and authentically our own? Are they subjective and ungrounded or are they in harmony with Tao, with natural law and the intelligence of the universe?

What is missing in our current economic system, and what would allow it to function more effectively, is a central value that can encompass everything that can be transacted, something that can be used to assign the proper relative value to everything transacted within the system.

What could be the central value that could embrace the diverse values of the world and promote understanding and coexistence among them? We are not talking about the Euro or the U.S. dollar but something more universal, a guiding principle that everyone can agree upon beforehand and against which the value of all products, whether material or nonmaterial, can be judged. What would such a central value be?

MEANING OF RECALIBRATION
IN A GLOBAL COMMUNITY

Until now, we humans have placed ourselves—and celebrated ourselves!—as the final arbiter of all living things on Earth, and organized our world accordingly. We have dealt with others, and with the Earth, under the premise that we are separate individuals, at war with one another and the world, surviving through ceaseless competition, our standards of value at the whim of ever-changing trends, caprices, manipulations, and even personal emotions and mood. Such was the limit of our value system. Such is the life that we lead today.

If human beings are too subjective and full of themselves to be objective judges of values, then what about the sciences, long thought to be objective? Or religions? Or even politics?

Relatively speaking, science can provide reliable standards to verify truth in a physical, material sense, but values are not its strength. Through study of the history of science, we know that science, like other system of knowledge, is not free from bias. And the truths of science are an ever-changing, ever-evolving body of information and knowledge. What one generation takes to be true is debunked and made obsolete by new discoveries as we proceed from partial knowledge to more complete knowledge. Any scientist will be the first to admit that despite all the great progress we have made in understanding our universe, our knowledge is far from complete.

Religions, on the other hand, purport to reveal the everlasting truth. Yet, as we all know, despite claims of universality and absolute authority, each religion, and the god or gods that it upholds, seems to have validity and power only for a certain nation or people, not for everyone. We don't yet have a single representative god of Earth, or a religious scripture or behavioral code accepted by all peoples and cultures.

How about the concepts of justice and freedom, whose pursuit is lauded as a universal human trait? What we see in the world is that one sense of freedom fights against another and one sense of justice strikes another. This is because even freedom and justice are subject to the interpretation of a particular group or people. One culture's "freedom" is another's unbridled license, and one culture's "justice" may appear as harsh and cruel when considered from a different cultural standpoint.

Thus, we see a world filled with confused and conflicting values, ideologies, and dogma that create dissension, conflict, and even violence and war, all because of the different-colored lenses worn by different groups. In a word, everything, including the self-proclaimed universal truths of natural sciences, religions, and politics, is trapped within the cage of a biased value system, conditioned by our long-worn colored lenses. We need a bigger view.

How much time did it take for human beings, descendants of monkeys with an advanced intellectual potential, to progress from their initial appearance on Earth and wondering at the mysteries of the stars, moon, and sun, to realize that they were not at the center of the cosmos? In the beginning, it was probably humiliating and terrifying to relinquish the notion that the universe revolved around them. Now this understanding is seen as evidence for the maturity of human awareness.

It's time to once again present evidence for our continuing

growth. We need another Copernican Revolution. To make such a revolution, we have to rethink our relationship to the Earth. We usually call everything that we relate to "ours" as if we have ownership over the object. Planet Earth is not an exception. With our mentality, it seems that we believe we have the right to use the planet any way we want. Do we even have the ability to protect the planet, let alone the right to use it? In the relationship between a part and the whole, if a part persistently tries to control the whole inharmoniously, it will be removed from the whole before it destroys the whole. This has happened repeatedly in the history of this planet.

If we scale down the 13.7-billion-year history of this planet to 14 years, human civilization is only 3 minutes, and the modern age is only 6 seconds. Some species such as dinosaurs had been dominant for incomparably longer periods of time than human beings. The greatest legacy of the dinosaurs for all other species, especially for mammals, was their dying, because by dying they opened up another stage of evolutionary drive for biological diversity that they were holding back for 160 million years, which is more than 50 times longer than the entire evolutionary history of the human species. If we see our relationship to this planet in a wide and long perspective, one thing is very clear: we belong to this planet, not the other way around, and the only way we can protect ourselves and thrive is by learning how to live with the whole in harmony.

We are part of the vast circle of life that inhabits this planet. At the center or basis of this circle of life is the Earth. The central standard of value for all life-forms here on Earth should be Earth herself, not our egos, needs, wants, and prejudices. We can use

Earth as the standard by which to judge all actions transacted on our planet. From such a point of view, we all are Earth citizens before we are a part of any group, nation, or religion.

If there were no Earth, then no altars could exist for you to worship your god. Even more, *you* wouldn't exist, nor your religion. Without Earth, no nation would exist, nor political ideologies with which to rule a nation. To recover the purest Zero mind, and cosmic consciousness, we first have to attain an Earth consciousness.

The Earth is the source of life for all forms of life. This entitles Earth, the long-term health and well-being of the Earth, to be the primary value, the most important consideration that all other values should be referred to for measurement. It is the common ground for all the values we pursue in our lives, personally and collectively. Despite its obvious importance, this common ground and primary value has been unappreciated and abused, and now is at serious risk. We have to revise and recalibrate our value systems based on the obvious primary value, our Earth.

PERSONAL APPLICATION OF RECALIBRATION

There are many different ways to apply the idea of recalibration in our everyday lives. Generally speaking, applying this idea means recovering natural balance in our body and mind, and finding how to do things in simpler and more natural ways, with less effort and input. However, what we usually mean by "less effort" typically involves using machines to work for us. This may mean "less" if we see it through our personal eyes, but when seen from the perspective of the whole, it is not less, it's a lot *more*.

In every product, large or small, that we own, use, or consume in our daily life, there's almost invariably water and energy—in one form or another (usually oil)—in amounts hundreds of times the size of the object. Vast amounts of energy and other resources are involved in production, and mountains of waste are generated.

To make it worse, substantial portions of these often non-renewable resources are not actually being used but instead are wasted, sometimes entirely, without having a single chance to reach the consumer's hand. In many other cases, they are wasted by not being used to improve the quality of life for people but instead to actually deteriorate it. So one obvious way we need to recalibrate our lives is to minimize the waste of resources that supports our lifestyle. In pursuit of a more natural life, perhaps we ought to sit a little less and sweat a little more.

This approach would involve a conscious shift from the pursuit of "more" toward appreciating the value of "less." This would mean taking a stand that goes contrary to the pressures of our consumer society. What I mean is that in our prevailing value system, which posits endless external growth as a key goal, "more" means good and "less" means bad. More, bigger, higher, and faster are the terms typically used to define what is good and valuable. This perspective is still dominant in most areas of our life, even when "more" actually means more devastation of our natural environment and greater possibility to destroy our civilization. This has to change, and each of us can play a role in the transition.

Two factors that are leading people to rethink the pursuit of "more" are debt and body weight, because nobody would think having more of these to be a positive. These two, being direct results of the drive for "more," are currently affecting most of the people in many countries. People desperately need *less* of these, and the only way to accomplish that is by doing less of what they have been doing; that is, by consuming less (buying fewer products, driving less and burning less fuel, and so on) and eating less.

The change from "more" to "less" means going back to basics, trying to find answers in doing less instead of more. For example, can you guess what animals in nature do when they are sick? Most commonly, they stop eating. Even domesticated animals, if they maintain their natural sense of balance, do the same. They stop putting food into their bodies. I'm not advocating that everyone should practice fasting! But I do want to say that if we find that something is not going well with our life, instead of running around looking for fixes and reaching out to others for help, why not pause, and even for a little while, stop doing what we've been doing, which, after all, has led to the current problem?

RECALIBRATION FOR HEALTH

After teaching around the world for so many years and meeting thousands of people, it is plain to me that one of the most vital areas of life that cries out for recalibration is our personal health. Or, put more directly, we need to rethink the way we live, because it is often our lifestyle habits that are creating health problems for millions of people.

What are the most basic things that we need to do well in order to live a healthy life? If you chose only three, what would they be? I would choose breathing well, eating well, and sleeping well. Exercise can be optional. It is good, and needed, but it is not as essential as these three. I have seen people who manage their lives pretty well without much exercise, but I have never seen people who can live well without breathing, eating, and sleeping well. No exception.

Breathing Well

How long can a person survive without eating? Whether through intentional fasting or being trapped somewhere without access to food, a human body has the capacity to survive for up to several weeks without eating. How about drinking? Probably about a week or less. And breathing? We all know that it would be very short. Even one or two minutes of suspension of oxygen supply will cause damage to your brain.

Breathing is literally our life, which started with a breath and will end when we cease to breathe. We will learn more about breathing later in this book, but it is important to know that simply by improving our breathing, we can substantially improve our physical and mental health. If your desire is to be healthy and improve your health in natural ways without resorting to medications, surgery, or other external support unless you really have to, your breathing is the first thing you need to address. Breathing well means breathing more slowly and deeply. The first step to achieve this is simply to become aware of your breathing.

I think my job is very interesting, or even weird, because I teach breathing. The fact that I have been successful demonstrates how far off we are from the natural balance of life—so far that we have even forgotten how to breathe naturally! There are many techniques of breathing. You may find some of them useful, but the simple guideline for breathing well is to breathe slowly, deeply, and comfortably. Just relax, feel your breathing, and breathe comfortably. Once you become aware of your breathing, it naturally becomes deeper and slower.

While you are enjoying your natural breathing, it improves the circulation, refreshes your energy, clears your mind, calms your emotions, and enhances your concentration. You become able to think more clearly, develop the power of attention and action, and improve the quality of your life.

Eating Well
As we all know, eating right is a challenge for almost everyone in our society, and there is a long list of health issues related to eating, from anorexia to obesity. What makes the situation more challenging is that the available information about healthy eating is often inconsistent and even conflicting. Do we need to drink whole milk or skim milk? Is milk good at all? Which is the main culprit in weight gain, carbohydrates or fat? Does the

human body need animal protein or do we just like it? These are just a few examples of recent controversies. And it gets even more complicated when we discover that much of the research supporting various claims comes from industry: research touting the benefits of milk may come from the dairy industry; research exposing the "dangers" of natural food supplements may originate from grants given by pharmaceutical companies; and so on.

In considering food and eating, it will be helpful to begin, as we learned with breathing, by becoming aware of what we eat and how we eat. By becoming aware of what we eat and how our body responds to the food we take in, we can gain feedback that will allow us to adjust our eating to our body's ever-changing conditions and needs with flexibility, instead of being overwhelmed and stressed by trying to stick to a rigid diet plan. By tuning in and listening with conscious awareness to your body, you will find, for example, that certain foods make you feel heavy, dull, and sleepy, while others help you feel light, fresh, and energetic. Different people with different physical constitutions thrive on different foods. The more you pay attention, the more you will learn about what is good for *you*.

Becoming aware of *how* we eat is also important. If you are not aware, what happens is that most of the time, you are not choosing your food because of what your body needs, but out of desires and cravings, or out of habit. Or to assuage an emotional upset. Or because that's what other people around you are eating. You may think you don't have time to sit quietly even for a few minutes and really enjoy your food—you have to get back to work, or type emails in between bites, or catch up on the latest news. But by becoming aware of how you eat, your eating will become a rich experience blessed with tasteful favor, joyful texture, a deep sense of gratitude, and pleasurable contentment. That's how eating becomes really eating, instead of throwing things into your mouth to fill your stomach with stuff that you don't really need or appreciate.

As with breathing, healthy eating begins with consciousness—being aware of what you are doing.

Sleeping Well

It is really a mystery why we need so many scientific studies, theories, products, and medications for a most natural zero-effort activity that all life-forms are entitled to: sleeping. If you do the first two things, breathing well and eating well, your sleep will also be better. If you want something more specific, then practice emptying your mind and body before sleeping.

Emptying your body is simple. You can achieve it by not eating for a few hours before you go to sleep and remembering to take a pee. Emptying your mind is not that easy—not because it is intrinsically difficult, but because we are making it not easy. There are of course issues, problems, responsibilities and duties that we have to take care of in our personal and professional lives. They are unavoidable. But this doesn't mean that we have to carry them into our sleep. There's not much that you can do about them while you are sleeping anyway.

When you're thinking about these things in your bed, most of the time what's really happening is that you are going over the same ground, repeating the same ideas, options, or questions over and over again. Most likely, you will think about these same things again the next morning. If you're really worried that you won't remember, there's a simple solution: instead of running over them in your mind and futilely carrying them into your sleep, just jot them down and consult your notes when you start a new day.

While you are sleeping, you have no need, not only for the thoughts you're dwelling on, but also everything else other than your body and your breath. As I suggested in chapter two, we need a functional ego to perform as a responsible social being, even after we have realized the truth of what we really are, but that's not what we need while we are sleeping. While sleeping, we're free to be what we really are, nothing more, nothing less.

So before you sleep, remember what you really are and experience yourself as what you really are by recognizing the vast space inside you, and feeling the Energy-Consciousness, LifeParticles, overflowing through the space and through your body. With this simple practice, you can sleep as what you really are, not as your name, jobs, duties, stresses, and all the burdens that you carry on your back during the day.

If you sleep with an empty body and empty mind, your empty mind will be filled with the peace and wisdom of Nothing, and your empty body will be recharged by the vital energy of LifeParticles during your restful sleep.

Breathing well, eating well, and sleeping well are very simple, but sometimes are not that easy to practice in the set patterns of our daily life. A break from the patterns in a comfortable but fresh environment is helpful, especially for the initial experiences. For this reason, I wanted to create a place where people could relax and dedicate some time for reflection on who or what they really are, get reconnected to Nature, and reinstate the natural rhythm of life in these basic and essential life functions. As I explained in my other books, I searched for a location across the country and found a good one near Sedona, Arizona. This is one of the reasons that we founded Sedona Mago Retreat about 15 years ago. This place was created to educate people about the principles of Tao, and help them integrate those principles into their personal lives.

Since then I have witnessed that even when people are far out of balance, they can recover their natural rhythm and balance once they allow themselves to open and allow the subtle energy of life to flow through them. When they recovered their natural sense of life, they felt connected to other people and all other life-forms and spontaneously wanted to do good to them.

Knowing what you really are, doing basic things well, and living with the genuine intention to benefit all . . . , if somebody asks how we can live by the principles of Tao, I would say this is the way.

If you have any health concern, I would suggest that you check these three basic things first and make sure you are doing them well before you go for any other more drastic or invasive measures. You may have health issues that require medication or surgery. Even if that's the case, if you breathe properly, eat wisely, and sleep peacefully, you will improve your condition more effectively. On the other hand, if you are not doing these basic things well, no matter what you do to improve your condition, eventually it won't work. The condition will resurface sooner or later because the foundation remains unchanged.

THE BEGINNING OF TRUE EARTH MANAGEMENT

The reevaluation and recalibration we have been discussing is just the tip of the iceberg. Once you begin to look within and around you, using the principles I've suggested, you will see the need for revision and renewal in every phase and facet of our lives, individual and collective. There is much work to be done, and we are the ones privileged to do it.

The key ideas of recalibration that apply across the board are recognizing inner space and pure consciousness as the foundation of all perception; recovering natural balance in all aspects of life; and establishing Earth and the wholeness of life on our planet as the central value and reference point in all our transactions and relationships.

I recall seeing a sign in a national park that read, "Please take with you what you brought and leave what was here already." This should be the basic axiom when dealing with Earth. Earth is not ours to do with as we please. We did not—and could not—purchase Earth with money. We have just been granted temporary stewardship. What we ought to aim for during our short time on Earth is not acquiring more land nor building higher skyscrapers, but attaining inner maturity, becoming complete human beings.

We all learned in kindergarten to put our toys back in their place once we were done playing with them. What the child gets out of playing with a toy is not the toy itself, nor the temporary emotional delight, but the maturity he or she gains from the experience. The child soon outgrows the toy and lets it go. If he/she doesn't, and seems too attached to the toy even into higher grades, we would recognize this as a worrisome sign of possible emotional or mental disturbance or imbalance.

We are currently too attached to our worldly toys, rather than to the lessons our playing could impart to further the maturity of our collective soul. We have been granted permission to use the resources of Earth in all their glorious abundance for our education and growth in life, and we have a responsibility to return them to their rightful place, as much as possible in their original condition.

Such awareness should be the basic minimum that guides our actions. If we base politics and economy upon this minimum, then politics becomes Earth-politics and the economy becomes Earth-economy. When this minimum becomes the ruling policy of the land, that will be the beginning of Earth management in its most genuine sense.

CHAPTER SIX

Your Creative Mind and Awakened Brain

WHAT NOTHING GIVES YOU

Recognizing Nothing as one's true nature, following the guidance of our conscience—the absolute truthfulness that comes
from Nothing— having a clear distinction between absolute and
relative values, and using the Earth as the external absolute scale
that matches the internal absolute truthfulness. This is where
we have come on our journey together through these pages.
How does this description sound to you? If it sounds close and
natural to you, and if you can resonate with it, I would say it
means your consciousness has gone through an unimaginable
transformation during this conversation. You may well be proud
of yourself even though your true nature, Nothing, doesn't have

anything to feel attached to, or proud of.

However, this is not yet the destination that I desired you to reach. You may have found this journey delightful and liberating, but actually the most exciting part is just about to begin. So far, our conversation has been about knowing and being, more specifically knowing what we really are and being it in reality. From this point on, the journey is about creating—creating the changes that we desire in our personal lives, creating the reality that we desire to experience, and eventually creating the world that we wish for ourselves, others, and the generations to come.

THOUGHTS BECOME THINGS: REALLY?

What do you think is the greatest contribution that quantum physics has made to our lives? It's a tough question to answer. Computers, lasers, transistors, medical imaging technology, CDs and DVDs, and many, many more inventions are based on the application of the duality of matter as waves and particles, and couldn't have come into existence without the discoveries of modern physics. But aside from these technological wonders, the greatest contribution may well be the scientific corroboration that observation by the conscious mind has the power to turn possibilities into reality. Even though the full implication of this understanding has yet to be revealed, it has given rise to the popular beliefs expressed as The Law of Attraction, or The Secret.

We all want to find the key to turning our desires and dreams into reality, the secret to utilizing the theory that "thoughts become things." Proponents of the Law of Attraction advocate the power of positive thoughts, which, they say, will act like magnets to bring results your way. Similarly, followers of The Secret will say, "Hold your desires firmly in mind—for your soul mate, financial success, better health, or whatever is important to you—and it will manifest in your life." These teachings imply, or state boldly, that you can make things happen just by holding ideas or images of what you desire in your mind.

The problem is that this secret doesn't appear to work for everybody. So you may find yourself wondering, "If the principles of quantum physics apply to everything, if it's true that observation by the conscious mind has the power to turn possibilities into reality, why doesn't my observation, my attention, affect or change things around me?"

In response, I would ask you two questions:

1. Is it truly a good thing for you if your thoughts become things?
2. Do you really observe?

Is It Truly a Good Thing for You If Thoughts Become Things?

This question reminds me of a story I heard when I was young:

There was a tree in a village. Although it looked just like other trees, it was actually a special kind of tree. It was a wish-fulfilling tree. Whatever you might say or think that you want when you sat under the tree would come true.

One day a traveler who was thirsty and hungry sat under

the shady tree. Not knowing that it was a wish-fulfilling tree, the traveler wished he had a glass of water to quench his thirst. Even before he recognized his own wish, a glass of clear, fresh water came up before him from nowhere. Because he was so thirsty, he drank the water without giving much thought to it.

Now that his thirst was gone, he realized how hungry he was and almost unconsciously thought how good it would be to have a hot meal. The moment he thought about it, a table with a delicious hot meal was spread out before him. He was certainly surprised but ate the food anyway.

When he had finished eating, he began to feel frightened. What, after all, was happening here? How could this be possible? "What if some evil ghosts are playing tricks on me?" he thought. Can you guess what happened? Yes, evil ghosts appeared, looking as fierce as his fearful imagination made them look. And then the poor traveler said to himself, "I am so scared. These ghosts will kill me." And sure enough . . .

So, "thoughts become things" can be good only if you are aware of your thoughts and you are able to think the way you choose. That means selecting from the constant stream of thoughts only the ones you approve and feel are worthy of entertaining and acting on. Otherwise, if your thoughts automatically materialized—could you handle it?

Imagine that there's a machine that can read your mind and immediately display and vocalize all your thoughts and mental images, like a movie, so that people around could see and hear every thought in your head. Would you be comfortable with that? And what would people think? I guess they might believe you were crazy!

There are so many wild thoughts running through our minds. Look at all the sci-fi movies, comics, and video games produced by our imagination. In our minds, we have extinguished the entire population of the world hundreds of times, destroyed the Earth, and annihilated galaxies, not to speak of the personal mayhem we have mentally unleashed on other drivers, aggressive salespeople, politicians, and so many others!

Would you agree that "thoughts become things" is potentially good but that there's an enormous risk that most of us are not ready to take yet? I would suggest that before we ask the cosmos for the power to have all our thoughts manifest, we need to train ourselves to become more aware, or mindful, of our thoughts, and we must become able to think comprehensively and wisely enough to use this power for the benefit of all.

Do You Really Observe?

Consider the intensity with which scientists observe the fine quantum particles. Scientific news and reports tell us about the process: the collider that is several miles in diameter, the massive amount of energy used to run the equipment, several thousand scientists involved in the study . . . This is the level of concentration and intensity that we invest for the observation of particles so tiny and sensitive that their physical state can be changed even by small changes in other factors and conditions involved in the process of observation.

This doesn't mean all quantum events require such intensity of observation, but at least it has been known that sustained observation has the effect of maintaining a given physical state of the object being observed. Given that you desire to change things in your life much bigger than the particles, how long do you maintain your observation and how much mental power do you invest in observing those things?

Even while you were reading this one paragraph, how many different thoughts ran across your mind? A Buddhist teacher said that three thousand thoughts may run across our mind at a single moment. Some of us may want to call this multitasking, but it has been confirmed that the human brain is not wired for multitasking. It can only focus on one thing at a time. What looks like multitasking is actually quick shifts of attention from one object to another. Whoever has experience working in a committed profession of any kind knows how important sustained, one-pointed attention is in determining the quality of the product you create and the integrity of the service you render.

So before we complain that our observation doesn't bring the desired result, we need to ask "Do I really observe?" If you discover that in fact you don't, the first step will be bringing your attention back to now and being present in the present moment.

CONSCIOUSNESS, AWARENESS, AND ATTENTION

Observing is not just seeing. It is watching with attention. Even though consciousness, awareness, and attention are often used interchangeably, we need to make a distinction among these three.

Consciousness is the foundation of all our experiences of being alive and being sentient. Through the discoveries of modern physics, we have recognized it to be deeply embedded in reality, an indispensable agent in all manifestation of physical reality in the universe. In other words, instead of being a phenomenon limited only to an individual brain, arising from neuronal interaction, consciousness has the capacity to create changes in the state of things in nature. This discovery suggests its property as a type of energy. As was explained in previous chapters, this agrees with the view of reality in the age-old tradition of Tao.

Within the scope of human cognitive experience, consciousness, when perceived, becomes awareness. We have consciousness as part of our nature as sentient beings, but this doesn't mean that we are aware at a particular moment. By perceiving our consciousness—becoming conscious of consciousness by a kind of self-referral "trick" that only humans seem to be capable of—we become aware. Awareness is the qualia of consciousness. Like other qualia, you cannot know it by understanding the concept or meaning. You know it only by really experiencing it. You know what awareness is only when you are aware. Awareness is the perception of your presence in the now.

Awareness in its pure state is nonlocal; there's no focal point in it. It is unbounded. Awareness, when managed and directed, becomes attention. By turning into attention, awareness becomes localized, and attains a focal point. Because of this feature, attention has the power to direct energy.

One of the simplest examples is the increase of the temperature of your skin by concentration. If you maintain your focus on your palm, you can experience the increase of skin temperature of your palm because maintained concentration brings the increase of blood flow and energy circulation to the body part. Trained meditators are known to keep their body sweaty hot even in a freezing temperature. This shows how attention creates and directs energy. More generally, we use attention in our action, and that's how we put energy into the action. Attention has its most powerful expression in purposeful action.

Let's imagine an archer in the Olympic games. In order to qualify to play in the games, she has to be a living, sentient human being, so she has consciousness. Before the games, there are lots of things coming and going in the space of her consciousness, such as excitement, expectation, fear, worries, memories of the painful training. . . . So she is not in the now, and therefore, she is not truly aware yet.

But the moment she stands on the archery field, she begins to feel her breathing, which occurs only in the present moment. By feeling her breathing, she becomes aware. She is aware of herself, the breeze, the sunlight, other players and spectators.

When it becomes her turn to shoot, she focuses on the target. At this moment, she is not aware of anything around her except the target. Her awareness has become attention. Her attention reaches its climax when she releases the arrow from her bow. The arrow is loaded not only with the power of her muscle, but also, more importantly, with the power of her attention. This power of attention manifests as a physical reality when the arrow hits the center of the target.

THE LAST, BUT NOT THE LEAST ADDITION: ACTION

Thoughts become things? True, but that analysis is not complete and is therefore misleading, because it gives the impression that you can make thing happen just by having an idea in your mind. To make it complete, we need to add two more words: thoughts become things *through energy*.

The first step is the energy you use consciously to generate and focus on the thought or image, which means attention. But how else do you use energy? What's the most obvious way of using energy? What do you do if there is something that you really want? I bet you wouldn't sit still and use your energy just for holding an image in your mind. I believe that you'd definitely jump to your feet and do something!

We use energy through action, whether physical, mental, or spiritual. Action is not something that just happens or you do by accident. Action is something that you do purposefully with attention. If you really want something, you will use as much energy for it, and you will use it through action.

To be brief and complete: thoughts become things through action. The most powerful tool for creating changes in your life is attention and action. No action means no creation.

BECOMING A CREATIVE OBSERVER

Observation by conscious mind has the capacity to create change. Each and every one of us has this capacity. Therefore, having the power is not the point. Using the power is the point. To make a clear distinction, I call the mind that can use this power a *creative observer.*

Even though consciousness doesn't seem to be confined to the human brain within the skull, we do experience consciousness through our brain. The transformation of consciousness to attention is facilitated by your brain. Driving thoughts into action is also processed by your brain. Your brain is the seat of the creative observer inside you.

How powerfully and effectively the creative observer inside you does its job depends on how integratively the functions and components of your brain are connected. For example, do you manage your thoughts or do random, crazy thoughts pop up all the time on their own? Do your emotions support you or do they sabotage you? Are your intentions put into action immediately or do you struggle with the intentions even after you have made the choice?

Unsustained and wavering focus, low energy, negative emotions, compulsive negative thought patterns . . . , these prevent you from using the full power of the creative observer. To help the creative observer work at full power, you need to retrain your brain.

THIS IS HOW YOU RETRAIN YOUR BRAIN

The reason we can retrain our brain is because the brain's neuronal networks are changeable according to our experiences, perceptions, thoughts, and emotions. The human brain's capacity for change in response to our experiences and activities is called neuroplasticity. The fact that we can change our brains is perhaps the most useful and optimistic bit of information any of us can have.

In her bestselling book, *My Stroke of Insight: A Brain Scientist's Personal Journey*, Harvard-trained neuroanatomist Jill Bolte Taylor wrote that thanks to the neuroplasticity of our brain cells, "their ability to shift and change their connections with other cells, you and I walk the earth with the ability to be flexible in our thinking, adaptable to our environment, and capable of choosing who and how we want to be in the world.

"I view the garden in my mind as a sacred patch of cosmic real estate that the universe has entrusted me to tend over the years of my lifetime." Dr. Taylor continued, "Once I consciously take over the responsibility of tending my mind, I choose to nurture those circuits that I want to grow, and consciously prune back those circuits I prefer to live without." Consciously tending your inner garden starts from realizing yourself as a gardener. When you have a vision or a picture that you desire to make your garden look like, your gardening can be more joyful and rewarding.

Here are the five steps I propose to retrain your train to make it more creative, peaceful, and productive:

1. Sensitize Your Brain

Open yourself up to new experiences. There is more to life than what you have known so far. This means awakening and enhancing the senses to become able to notice the subtle movements and changes that happen in body and mind. It can be compared to feeling buoyancy as you learn to swim, or feeling the response of your vehicle to the movement of your hands and feet in order to learn to drive. When you experience new sensations and new and unfamiliar sensory input, new areas of your brain become awakened. By concentrating on these perceptions, dormant areas of the brain become enlivened and activated.

2. Make Your Brain Flexible

Challenge yourself to come out of your comfort zone. Becoming able to see things differently brings new insights and creativity. The brain is actually the most flexible organ in a physical sense. It doesn't have any bone or muscle. It's like soft tofu. As soft as it may be, however, it is in some ways the most resistant organ in our body because of what used to be considered "hard-wired" habits and beliefs. Habits and beliefs exist in the brain in the form of neural circuits or networks, which are strengthened by repetitive use.

But the reality of neuroplasticity, the ability of the brain to continually renew itself and rewire its neural connections, is now beyond dispute, which means we can always learn something new and change old patterns of thinking and acting. Brain Versatilizing is the process to make the brain circuitry more malleable through stimulation, and by trying out new behaviors beyond our habitual comfort zone. We can develop a more resilient attitude through this process and become able to deal with challenges more creatively.

3. Refresh Your Brain

Recover the Zero Point. What's on your scale, weighing you down? How can you make a right decision if your scale is not attuned to zero? Reevaluate the information that you have in your brain. We all have an enormous amount of information there. Some pieces, like our names, are retrieved easily, and others are stored below our conscious awareness. Some, like habits and beliefs, are well-traveled highways of brain circuitry, difficult to change.

The important thing is that information is information, not reality. Information is for use; it is not meant to be the master. Realizing this is the beginning of Brain Refreshing. It puts information in its proper place as a resource, and restores consciousness to its natural state, uncontaminated by information. Through this process, body and brain also recover their natural balance, and natural healing usually occurs as a result.

4. Find Your Primary Value and Build Integrity

The core of the operating system for your brain is the primary value that you pursue. Do you have one? If you do, do you really live by it? Does your life demonstrate this value? Earn trust from your brain by doing what you said you would do. Then, your brain will serve you fully and you can use your brain functions, such as imagination, intention, emotions, and desires in an integrative way. Instead of each of these functions trying to move in different directions, all of them will work together for a single goal. This is how we can use our brain most effectively and utilize the true power of our mind and consciousness.

5. Use Your Brain as Its Master

When we are able to use our brain functions integratively, we can use our brain and the power of consciousness for a purpose that is big enough to benefit all. By living for such a purpose, we realize the full potential of our brain and of what we really are. This last step is not part of the process of training your brain. It is living, living truly as the master of your life and your brain. It is a life of making choices, not from any relative or external conditions but from your true nature—putting your energy into action without inner struggle and creating the result as you intended. It is creative and productive life in its deepest and greatest sense.

THE POWER OF MEDITATION

You may be a committed meditator, a beginner, or perhaps you've just heard about it, and thought it might be a good idea to give it a try. Whether you practice it consciously or not, we are all meditators in a sense, because self-reflection comes from the very nature of consciousness. If practiced intentionally and purposefully, meditation is a powerful way to enhance your attention, to develop your ability to think mindfully, and to use the unlimited creative potential of your mind.

Your conscious mind, when it is not disturbed by any

stimulation from inside or outside—any thought or sense perception—reflects on itself and becomes aware of itself. Consciousness becomes aware of its own nature. This usually brings the expansion of the capacity of your mind, which enables you to see things with fresh perspective and ask new questions.

You may experience this inner silence even during the busy hours of your daily life. Out of nowhere, it seems, there's an unexpected pause and stillness in our mind, and we ask ourselves, "What is this? What's going on? Why am I doing this? Is this important in my life?" Usually we don't carry this questioning very far. We stop ourselves and go back to work, saying, "What am I doing?" with a slightly different tone this time.

When you have some quiet time to think, you may revisit these questions and sometimes you'll have meaningful insights about yourself and life. Asking fundamental questions, and reflecting on yourself like this can be a powerful meditation, even though you don't sit in a half-lotus pose, light a candle, or burn incense.

For more committed, "formal" meditation, below are some guidelines that apply to all types of meditation practices and all purposes.

Calm Your Mind

Make your mind quiet and clear of disturbing thoughts and emotions. You can achieve this by focusing on the feeling of subtle energy on your palms, inside your body, and all around.

What's in your mind now? Is it calm and peaceful or is it crowded and messy with busy thoughts and stressful emotions? Or are you even aware of what's going on? If you look, chances are good that you'll find lots of information running through your mind, affecting not only how you feel now but also how you will live in the future, because these bits of information and gusts of emotions shape the way you see the world, and the way you respond to the challenges and opportunities of life. Don't you want a little more control over what happens in your mind? Don't you want moments of peace and restful breaths? Don't you want to clear your mind and see things through fresh eyes? Meditation is an answer.

How do we meditate? It starts with being present. Meditation is not thinking about your past or future. Normally our mind is full of thoughts, either negative or positive. Most of our thoughts are about the past or future. When in the past and negative, you call them regrets; when in the past and positive, you call them good memories; when in the future and negative, you call them worries; when in the future and positive, you call them hope.

Our minds jump around these four spaces ceaselessly, rarely staying at the center, which is called Now. Is there any moment when your mind isn't preoccupied with one of these? Is your mind quiet even while you are sleeping? Even while you are sleeping, your dreams are composed of a mixture of some or all of these.

When you think your life is not proceeding exactly the way you wish, when it feels like there's something missing, when you feel lost and disoriented, that is the time you need to pause and see what's really happening in your life, inside and outside. This is what meditation is for. It all starts from being present.

Being present doesn't take any thought. You can just be. The only thing that you need in order to be present here and now is your breathing. Isn't that so? That's all you need, literally. When you feel your breath, where do you think your mind is? Your mind is with your body. The moment you feel your breath, you will notice your breath becomes slower and deeper. With your breath becoming slower and deeper, your mind also calms down.

Now, I need to explain something important. To those who don't practice breathing as a path to meditation, "deep breathing" usually means breathing fully, to the full capacity of the lungs, like when your doctor is listening to your chest and tells you to take a deep breath. But this is not recommended during meditation, because expanding the chest for deep breathing disturbs our quiet inner balance and therefore is not helpful for meditation, which is all about settling down.

As meditation deepens, breathing naturally gets softer, rather than deeper. But, at the same time, the location of the breath moves deeper into the body. The practitioner may start meditation with chest breathing, but as the meditation session advances, the breathing goes deeper down, to the lower abdomen, and this is how the breathing really becomes soft and quiet. The more a person practices meditation, the more readily the breath settles to this deeper level.

As one's breathing goes down to a deeper level, the diaphragm begins to be used for breathing more fully. This brings, on the other hand, the increase of total capacity of breathing without causing the disturbance of chest breathing. So the breathing becomes deep in multiple senses.

When your breath is slow and deep, and when your mind is calm, if you raise your hands and focus on your palms, you will begin to feel the subtle energy that connects your body and mind: LifeParticles.

Focus on your palms with your palms facing each other and feel the energy.

Let your hands slowly move away from each other and let them get close very slowly.

When you feel it, please remember that what you are feeling between your palms and what you really are, is one and the same thing: Energy-Consciousness. The entire universe, on its most fundamental level, is made up of the same thing. Through LifeParticles, all become one.

With these three—body, mind, and energy—integrated into one, you become whole, not scattered or fragmented anymore. With this, you stop being merely your name, your job, your title, your memory, your thoughts and emotions, and you become what you really are. You inhabit your wholeness.

Now you can put your hands down on your knees, and bring your attention down to your lower abdomen with a deep breath. Even after you finish this meditation practice, try to maintain the sense of energy on your palms and through your body. How do you feel? How's your mind? Do you feel the peaceful inner space overflowing with light and energy?

This is a simple, powerful technique of energy meditation. It is called *Ji-Gam* in Korean. *Ji* means "quieting," and *Gam* means "emotions." Together it means "quieting the emotions, and quieting the mind."

Attune Your Breathing

Breathing is the primary expression of the rhythm of life. Be aware of your breathing and breathe naturally. This will lead you into unity with the great flow of Life, your true nature.

Heartbeat, blood pressure, body temperature, sweating, breathing, all of these are vital functions regulated by the autonomic nervous system (ANS). *Autonomic* means "self-regulating," which is why we don't need to pay attention to these functions or need to regulate them intentionally. If you had to take care of your heartbeat consciously, so that it wouldn't stop if you didn't think about it, what else could you do in your everyday life? Thankfully, these are all autonomic and don't need our attention to work.

Now, among the vital functions regulated by the ANS, if one is different from the rest, which one do you think it is, and why?

Yes, breathing. Why? Because breathing is intentionally controllable. It is automatic, but it is also controllable. What about others, such as body temperature? You may be able to learn how to control your body temperature by practicing for a really considerable amount of time if you believe it is worthwhile. But it might be wiser to learn how to put on and take off your clothes or how to adjust the thermostat.

Breathing, while reflecting your inner physiological condition, can also affect it. Here's the possibility to use breathing as a powerful tool to manage your thoughts, emotions, and energy.

Breathing affects the balance of the autonomic nervous system, which is maintained by the interaction between the two subdivisions of the ANS, sympathetic and parasympathetic. Simply put, sympathetic excites you and parasympathetic calms you. To see how this works, put your index and middle fingers on your wrist to feel the pulse, or you can put your fingers on your neck under either side of your chin.

While you breathe comfortably, feel your pulse and try to

notice any difference between inhaling and exhaling. Within several breaths, you may find that the pulse becomes faster when inhaling and slows down when exhaling. Heartbeat speeding up means the dominance of the sympathetic subdivision, and slowing down indicates the dominance of the parasympathetic. That's how your breathing affects the ANS directly.

The autonomic nervous system is supposed to be in a natural balance, alternating between periods of rest and digestion, and times for dynamic or urgent action. However, in our current hectic lifestyle with so much stress and stimulation, our ANS is normally out of balance, with overactivity of the sympathetic and underactivity of the parasympathetic. As you may guess, breathing can be a powerful means to restore your ANS to its proper balance.

Because breathing rate influences the sympathetic dominance, and breathing depth influences parasympathetic dominance, the most effective way to recover the ANS balance is by breathing slowly (this calms down your overly excited sympathetic nervous system) and deeply (this powers up your tired parasympathetic nervous system). One cycle of breathing consists of four stages: inhaling, pause, exhaling, pause.

For adults in the state of rest or semi-activity, optimal breathing rhythm occurs at one cycle in 12 seconds, or five cycles in 1 minute. When operating at this pace, cardiopulmonary efficiency is maximized. Seven to ten cycles per minute mean mild excitement. Ten to twenty cycles per minute indicate a moderate level of stress. More than 20 cycles per minute mean you are under considerable stress. Of course there can be exceptions to this general rule, but breathing slowly and deeply will help everyone recover the healthy natural balance of the autonomic nervous system.

When you are stressed, first notice and acknowledge it. By doing so, you can use the space between the stressor and your reaction for different choices, instead of reverting automatically to your habitual responses. Become aware of your breathing, and breathe comfortably. As soon as you become aware of breathing, your breath naturally becomes deep and slow. Focus on each pause between inhaling and exhaling. It will give you a sense of space and quietude inside you. This sense of space and quietude will give you power and freedom to make a better choice, even in a situation that has caused you stress.

The deeper and slower your breathing becomes, the more space you will create inside you. Eventually, the space will become so big that all your thoughts and emotions look trivial and insignificant in the vastness of your inner space. That's how you can attain peacefulness inside, and recover your natural state, your true nature.

Breathing is the most natural and powerful way to balance your energy and enhance concentration. By attuning your breathing, you can become one with the natural rhythm of life that flows through you all the time. This is called *Jo-Shik*, a term for traditional energy meditation in Korean. *Jo* means "regulating," or "attuning," and *Shik* means "breathing."

Here's a poem I'd like to share as my reflection on breathing.

BREATH

The breath that I breathe is not mine
It is the breath of the universe
Breath of life
Swirling in the grand breath of Cosmic Mind
Sighing with the soft breathing of Cosmic Energy.
Grass, trees, clouds, people
All the universe dances
To the rhythm of my breathing.

I forsake my weary past
With expulsion of each breath.
With each breathing cycle
I die and am reborn.
I am no longer afraid of death
For death is the bright promise of new life.
I know that were I not to die
I could not be reborn into a new existence.

As I inhale and exhale
I see my existence anew
·And recognize the law of the Cosmos.
When I breathe freely
I become one with Heaven
One with the divine.
For I have never been apart
From the heaven, land, and sea.

Within this breath
You and I are one,
Not bound by time or space
Nor knowing sorrow and pain,
Living according to the law
Of heaven and earth,
Tasting the sky
Feeling the universe.

Drinking the energy of the universe
Breathing along with the Cosmos
With each breath
I am reborn
Into a brand-new existence.
With each breath
The universe begins again
With a brand-new wave.

Be Centered

Stay at the center of your being without allowing your attention to become distracted by sensory stimulation. Be still and let your true nature manifest and shine through.

For a deeper meditation, you may need to separate yourself from outside stimulation because, whether you like it or not, if there's stimulation, your senses will respond and cause an agitation, large or small, in your mind, breaking the inner stillness that you strive for. This is called *Geum-Chok* in Korean. *Geum* means "avoid," and *Chok* means "contact." In the traditional

Tao practice of Korea, people sometimes secluded themselves in a cave where they meditated with only minimal supplies to provide their bare physical needs. When your mind is still and undisturbed by stimulation, the true nature naturally shines out and you can directly see what you really are.

However, this doesn't mean everyone must have this experience. Whether you see it or not, your true nature is already there. Always. You don't have to go somewhere to get it, or become someone or something other than what you are. If it is our true nature, what else can we be? Of course having the direct experience of seeing and being it is precious. However, no matter how precious the experience is, it passes. What remains is the *big* understanding of reality as One and Nothing that embraces all and the willingness to give everything to benefit all. When you live by this big understanding and big heart, you are living an enlightened life. You can accept and live by this big understanding regardless of your level of experience. It is primarily your choice, and no matter how long you have practiced, and no matter how profound your experience was, it is still a choice.

Another thing that we need to know about this practice is that inner stillness cannot be achieved just by separating yourself from external stimuli. Please tell me whether you think your mind will become quieter or more noisy and messy if you seclude yourself in a cave for twenty-one days? If you have ever tried meditating, you know the answer. That's why we need Ji-Gam (quieting mind) and Jo-Shik (attuning breathing) before Geum-Chok (avoiding contact). Otherwise, the inner struggle will be unbearable even to those with a sinewy mind, and the result will probably be exactly the opposite of what you want to achieve.

In the tradition of Tao practice, only a fully enlightened teacher who can see whether a student is ready will tell the student to enter into the practice of Geum-Chok.

Practically, the idea of secluding oneself for several weeks for meditation is hard to implement in these times. One alternative is passion, a real burning passion. When you are extremely hungry, you will not think of anything but food. When you are really thirsty, everything that you have in your mind will be about water. Likewise, if you want something so much that your focus becomes one-pointedly sharp and stays stable all the time, you already have achieved Geum-Chok.

When I went into the mountain to get the answer to my question about my true identity, I didn't do it for the undisturbed isolation of Geum-Chok. I was already living a state of Geum-Chok before going to the mountain—my whole focus was concentrated on the question so much that all other things lost their meaning. I just needed a place where I could do everything possible to achieve my goal without bothering others or being bothered by others.

Likewise, if you want something so much that you don't forget it even for a moment and you maintain your focus all the time, it is Geum-Chok. Some people may have a similar worldly focus, an obsession with money-making or career advancement, but in the spiritual realm, for genuine Geum-Chok, one condition is needed: what you want should be something that can lead you to your inner greatness, your true nature. It should be its own purpose, not a means to get something else, such as money to live more comfortably. If this is the case, money is not the purpose. Living comfortably is the purpose. But I'm not sure whether you can develop such a burning passion just to live more comfortably. That's why it is so important to know what you really want.

What you really want is to realize what you truly are. Why? Because what you *truly are* is infinite intelligence and creativity, Energy-Consciousness, LifeParticles, which gives you the power and wisdom to attain fulfillment and completion in life.

MEDITATION FOR CONTEMPLATION AND CREATION

For most people, meditation is associated with relaxation and peace of mind, and these are the practical reasons many people seek out, learn, and practice meditation. However, relaxation and peace of mind are only half of the uses for meditation. The other, probably more important aspect, is for creation. To make a distinction, I would call these uses contemplative and creative, respectively.

Contemplative Meditation

In essence, contemplative meditation is quieting your mind, watching carefully, and finding out what's really happening. Whether you are just curious, want to use your time and energy more meaningfully, want to live more fully—or whatever interests you—finding out what's really happening is important. It's especially helpful for all the choices you make in your everyday life because the condition for making right choices is accurate information, knowing what's happening both inside and outside. Through contemplative meditation, you achieve a more pure observation and get insights about how to act in response to what happens.

In order to learn to use our mind, we need to enter our mind, just as we need to go into the water to learn to swim. That is what contemplative meditation is for. When you are dreaming, you are watching your consciousness. However, dreams arise involuntarily; you don't ordinarily have any control over the experiences in your dreams. Going into your consciousness consciously is like going into the water with scuba gear such as a diving suit, oxygen tank, mask, and fins. You can explore the lake of your consciousness and remove rubbish if you find some there.

What is most meaningful in this visit to your inner space is recognizing the space itself behind all images and thoughts you encounter. The final goal is to reach the state of the unity of Energy-Consciousness without any sense of myself as a separate being. This is the source of true insight and healing.

Creative Meditation

What's in your mind now? If you close your eyes, what do you see? When there's no thought or image, what is there? You may say nothing, but the vast emptiness you see as nothing is actually vibrating with limitless creative potential. I propose to call it MindScreen.

MindScreen is the space for creation. This is where LifeParticles—the unity of energy and consciousness, the primary stuff of creation—work. In your MindScreen, you the creator; MindScreen, the space for creation; and LifeParticles, the stuff that you use for creation, are one. What you see when you close your eyes is not just the back of your eyelids. It is the vast space of Energy-Consciousness, which is vibrating with limitless possibilities of creation. It is like a fertile land that is waiting for seeds to be sown.

This space of Energy-Consciousness is boundless and thus encompasses the entire universe. The stuff that you use for your creation is the same stuff that constitutes the universe. Therefore, when you use LifeParticles, you are using a language with which the entire universe can understand and resonate. When you create something in your MindScreen with LifeParticles, you are broadcasting your creative intention to the responsive universe. Your ideas, thoughts, and intentions are the seeds of creation, and your attention is the powerful tool that drives energy toward the object or outcome you want to create. Your positive emotion and passionate action add power to the creative process.

As I will explain below, you can develop your sensitivity to feel LifeParticles. By using the subtle sense, you can feel and direct the flow of LifeParticles in your MindScreen. It's like feeling the clay while shaping a figure with your hands. In the MindScreen, the hand, the clay, the figure, the image that you want to create, and the intention to create it are all one. Just as an artist, his/her tools, and the materials for creation work together in a genuine creative work, when you work with LifeParticles in your MindScreen; then, your intention, MindScreen, LifeParticles, and your creation all work together. They are different in form, but in essence, the same LifeParticles.

When you are deep into a creative meditation, sometimes you lose the sense of which one is which because everything moves in a harmonious resonance. Through Creative Meditation, you can have the tangible feeling of creation.

SIMPLE FLOW OF CREATIVE MEDITATION WITH LIFEPARTICLES

There are many different ways to practice Creative Meditation. The flow presented here is the simplest version that anyone can practice easily. The first two steps can be categorized as contemplative meditation to relax your body and calm your mind. You may stop there, or you can proceed to the next steps for Creative Meditation. Even though these are presented as steps to understand the process more clearly, there's no separation between steps. They are a single flow. Let's begin.

1. Assume a Comfortable Position

Assume a comfortable position, either sitting or standing, and begin by gently turning your head from side to side. Continue this turning while you also tap your lower abdomen lightly. This simple movement will relieve the tension from your neck and strengthen the energy center at your lower abdomen. This creates the energetic condition for optimal functioning of our body and brain: Cool Head, Open Chest, and Warm Abdomen.

2. Calm Your Breathing

Breathing slowly and deeply calms your mind and brings your attention to your body. Simply by becoming aware of breathing, your mind will be present in the now, since breathing is always occurring in the now. Counting your breaths can be helpful because to count your breaths, you need to be aware of your breathing. Count 10 breaths, and your breathing will naturally become deep and slow. Feel the emptiness at the pause between breaths. This will bring a state of relaxed concentration, enabling you to feel the subtle sense of energy.

3. Feel Energy

Slowly raise your hands in front of you, with palms facing each other. Focus on your palms and feel the subtle sense of energy. Remember that what you are feeling between your palms and what you really are, are one and the same—Energy, or LifeParticles. The entire universe, on its fundamental level, is made up of the same Energy-Consciousness. On that level of pure being, all are one. Play with the energy by slowly opening and closing your arms. Enhance and expand your sensation of the flow of LifeParticles from your hand to your arms to your whole body. Stay connected with the feeling of the flow.

4. Open Your MindScreen

Maintain the sense of LifeParticles on your hands and raise your hands, palms facing each other, up to the level of your forehead. Visualize a ball of LifeParticles like the sun between your hands. Feel the light and vibration of the Sun of LifeParticles flowing into your brain, and spreading down through your spine to your entire body. Expand the Sun of LifeParticles onto a screen. It is your MindScreen.

You are now in the creative space of consciousness. Visualize what you want to create on your MindScreen. Use the functions of all your senses. Imagine the sound, smell, and touch of your creation. Feel the tangible feeling of what you are creating by the sense of energy on your hands. It will be like shaping an object using clay or dough. Because your hand and energy work together in resonance, sometimes the distinction disappears, and all becomes one in the harmonious flow of LifeParticles.

For example, your hand moves, following the feeling of the flow of energy—but the movement itself also creates the flow. So sometimes it feels like your hand leads the process, and other times it feels like the energy flow guides your hand movement. During this dynamic exchange, the sense of separation vanishes, and the feeling of creation becomes clearer and more tangible.

5. Offer Your Prayer of Gratitude

Bring your hands together in front of your chest. Offer your gratitude for your creation. Remember how you attained everything that you have now. Having something started from wanting it. Didn't it? Wanting something is the beginning of the process of having it.

When you want something and you don't have it, it may be a cause of stress to you. However, if we reflect on how we came to have things that were not there originally, we can be excited, delighted, and grateful that we want something even before we have it. Seen from this perspective, wanting something—or more specifically, being able to want something while it is not there yet—is already a gift in itself. This is why we offer gratitude.

This is the simple flow of LifeParticle Meditation. It will take just about 5 to 10 minutes, so you can easily practice two or three times a day. This will help you stay focused on your goal with a positive attitude. This positive focus will help you align your actions toward achieving your goal. With this integration of attention and action, you can make things happen more effectively.

To help people visualize the LifeParticle Sun more easily, I created an image of the LifeParticle Sun. It can be used to enhance your concentration, and to direct the flow of LifeParticles with your mind. You may find this useful, especially when you send LifeParticles to other people to help them.

There are many suggestions about how to use MindScreen and LifeParticles, and more inspiring stories of success and healing, than I can possibly put in this book. You can visit www.LifeParticles.com for more ideas and information.

APPLICATION OF LIFEPARTICLE MEDITATION

Healing is one of the most powerful and widely beneficial ways of practicing the Creative Meditation, because effective healing requires concentration, positive energy, and creative visualization.

You can practice with yourself, with somebody else, or in a group. It is the same process. The only difference is what you do during the fourth step, MindScreen. During this step, you visualize the person(s) who need(s) healing and send them LifeParticles. You can do this with the person either present or at a distance.

If you are working in a group, everyone sits in a circle and one person who needs healing moves to the center. The person explains his/her condition and why he/she needs healing. All the people go through the first three steps, and in the fourth step, they send LifeParticles to the person inside the circle. Visualizing the details of the condition or the body parts of the person may be helpful but is not required. So you don't need to get stressed too much for the details of the visualization. Rather, stay relaxed and connected with the flow of LifeParticles, with the pure intention to heal. Visualize the person becoming brighter, healthier, and happier.

People who have participated in the practice of collaborative healing with LifeParticles, whether they were inside the circle or outside, report wonderful experiences of healing and awakening. This is because there is truly no giver or receiver: all participants are in one and the same flow of LifeParticles and are healed.

WHAT MAKES US GREAT?

The most precious discovery that people who practice LifeParticle healing with others gain from their experience, however, is not that we all have the power to heal within us, though of course that is a valuable revelation. The most precious discovery is that we have the natural intention to benefit other people, even strangers, without condition or expectation of return.

Desiring to heal oneself or to heal somebody close to you is so natural. You don't need greatness to do this. Even animals do it. No matter how well you do, there's no greatness in what you do if you do it just for yourself. It is not a bad thing, but we wouldn't say it is truly greatness. Then what is it that makes us great? To find the answer to this question, let's have a moment for reflection on our deepest desire for our life.

We know that life is uncertain. Nothing is permanent. However, no matter how uncertain our life is, there's one thing that is 100 percent certain, guaranteed, no exception. What is that? Yes, that we will die. You may not want to talk about this in your daily life. But sincere contemplation of this truth helps us find deeper meaning in life.

When you honestly face the fact that the time you will have in this body and this lifetime is limited, you begin to ask yourself important questions about how you will use that time. What legacy, what gift do you wish to leave behind for others? How would you like to be remembered after you have left this life? Please take some time for reflection with this question in your mind, and listen to what comes from the deepest part of your heart.

This exercise is not new. It has been practiced in many programs in many different ways, and even been used in scientific research about human behavior and attitudes. What emerges consistently from this research is that almost everyone—regardless of their life conditions, experiences, and backgrounds—wants to be remembered not just as a successful person but also as a person who helped others and benefited the world. Even though I already believed that everyone has this great mind and generous heart, it was still inspiring to learn about this research. Everybody has a deep desire to help others, and the question, "How do I want to be remembered after I leave this life?" when asked sincerely, has led them to hear the voice of this noble desire in their heart.

So, what makes us great? What makes us more than this small person in this fragile physical body? Through collaborative healing and our responses to the question of how we want to be remembered, I believe we have found the answer. We have the Noble Desire to help others and benefit the world, without expecting any return or recognition. What makes us great is not our knowledge, skill, money, or power. What makes us truly great is this noble desire, this passion that transcends all separation, that goes beyond one's limitations and wants to hug others and embrace the whole world. This is not something that we need to learn, because we already have it. It just needs to be acknowledged and awakened.

This is the same mind that I explained in the previous chapter: conscience, the Hong-Ik spirit, the true power to uplift and benefit the world.

DEVELOPING THE POTENTIAL OF THE HUMAN BRAIN

If we consider this noble desire to be of benefit to the world as the greatest attribute of humanity, it makes me wonder about our systems of education today. What is education really for? How well is it serving to develop this noble quality? Education, etymologically, means "bringing something out." It is based on the belief that humanity has good, positive, creative attributes as inherent potential, which, when nurtured and allowed to grow and develop, will benefit the person and the world. I believe this is the definitive essence and purpose of education. Going back to our earlier discussion about recalibrating, reconsidering, and reevaluating our values and priorities, I would suggest that developing in every student the positive potential that can benefit the world has to be the primary purpose of education, rather than the effort to impart knowledge and skills.

Is this what is happening in education now? I am very doubtful. I'm a parent of two sons and am grateful that they have grown up to be healthy, mature, and responsible. Because I didn't do as much for them as they wanted when they were young, there is always a sense of regret in my heart. Thankfully, they understood that their father was involved in work for the benefit of more than my family and myself, and that what I did would eventually benefit them, too. With this mixed feeling of gratitude and regret, I deeply share all parents' concern for their children, and I want to provide the best education possible for our next generation.

I have long believed that developing the greatness within, finding absolute truthfulness inside, recovering the power of conscience, and awakening the spirit of Hong-Ik was the way to help our young citizens find the meaning of life, and awaken their latent passion to do good things for the world and for all life.

Because I was not able to find many people who agreed with my belief—or if they did, did not do anything about it—I decided to attempt these educational reforms on my own. That's how I developed the concepts, principles, and practices of Brain Education. I started providing the programs of Brain Education and created a university in Korea to educate leaders and teachers to deliver Brain Education. The leaders of Brain Education are now working in many schools in the United States, Japan, Germany, and Korea. In the United States, Brain Education programs have been taught to more than 10,000 teachers and 30,000 students in nearly 350 schools. In collaboration with the United Nations, the Brain Education school program is also being delivered in many developing countries of Latin America, Africa, and Southeast Asia. (For more information about Brain Education, please visit www.ibreaus.org.)

That's not the end of the story. Actually, it is the beginning because, like many parents and others who feel responsible for the quality of life in our homes and communities, I believe good education is our future and hope for humanity.

The recent violence and tragedies in U.S. schools led many observers to say that the key to preventing any additional tragedies is to help young people find a deeper meaning of life. I totally agree, and I think this is far more important than creating more administrative procedures and regulations. What makes our job easier is the fact that our children already have this attribute in their hearts: the spirit of Hong-Ik, the inextinguishable passion to do good things for the world. We just need to guide them to find it. If people ask me what Brain Education is for, I would say it is for awakening this noble spirit.

CHAPTER SEVEN

Invitation to a Great Experiment

THE ILLUSION OF STABILITY

Between a skyscraper built with glass and steel on a concrete foundation, and a Native American tepee made with canvas and wooden poles and set up on bare land, which one looks more stable to you? Probably you'd say, "The skyscraper." The more energy a system uses and the more high tech it employs, the stronger and more stable it appears. However, the truth is exactly the other way around. The more energy a system uses, and the more it depends on high tech, the more vulnerable it is, and that vulnerability makes it less stable and ultimately less sustainable. That is our current system of living. Let me explain.

Could you maintain your life if all electricity were cut off?

For just a few days, you probably could. But after that? Walking up the stairs to your 40th floor office or your 10th floor apartment, working in a building with no openable windows and no power to run air-conditioning or ventilation for air flow, and no water to wash your hands or flush the toilet—it's unimaginable.

Remember Superstorm Sandy that devastated parts of the East Coast of the United States in late 2012? People couldn't get gas for their cars because the power went out, so the pumps didn't work. Without fuel, many couldn't drive to the supermarket, which was too far away to walk. Even if you could somehow make your way to the market, the shelves would soon be empty of food, because the trucks couldn't deliver it. You wouldn't be able to cook even if you had all the ingredients, since without power, the water pumps wouldn't be able to transport water to your home. How long do you think you could last under such conditions?

Nevertheless, our civilization is ceaselessly expanding and co-opting more and more of Earth into its territory. To maintain itself and grow, it is using more and more energy and material, making us sink deeper and deeper into its clutches. It's obvious to all of us who think about it that Earth cannot sustain such a pace for much longer.

And it isn't just luxuries that we'll have to do without. Our current system of living, wasteful and destructive, can't be maintained even at its most basic level. And by *basic* I mean truly basic—the air, water, and land that are increasingly polluted, food that is toxic and lacking in nutrition, and energy that is running out unless we learn to use renewable sources such as the sun and wind. Our entire system of living must inevitably change. If we don't make a choice now, sooner or later deteriorating conditions will force us to adapt to a new way of living, which will not only be far worse, but also difficult for us to adapt to because we won't be ready or prepared for such a change. This is why it is necessary for us to make the choice to change. Now.

SOFT BUT FUNDAMENTAL CHANGES

How can we change the system of living? If we were to attempt to change the whole social infrastructure in a day, the stress and strain of such an effort would probably destroy civilization itself. How can we turn this bus around without an abrupt stop that would throw everything into chaos?

The final goal we desire to achieve is eventually changing the direction of the current human civilization and re-creating a more balanced and sustainable one. This sounds daunting to anybody with a sane mind. Even just hearing the words "changing the civilization" coming out of the mouth of a mere single individual may make many people doubt the functionality of that person's brain.

However, I suspect the way we think of change of this magnitude and depth reflects the dominant paradigm of our current civilization. It shows that we think "hard." We think in terms of structures, systems, processes, control, regulations, resources, stress, resistances, costs, and so on. On the other hand, we know that the world, at the deepest, subtlest level, is not as solid as it looks. In fact, it is almost nonmaterial. So we need to change the way we think of reality.

We should think "soft." This is especially significant when we want to make meaningful changes in our lives. The deeper we go, the softer reality becomes—the less solid and structured. And that's where we start making changes, from the deepest and softest.

It's not the world that we need to change. It is the people who inhabit the world. It's not machines that we need to change. It is the people who use those machines. Even with people, we can start the change from the softer things such as the way we breathe, and the way we feel about or toward other people and other living beings. These soft parts shape our behaviors and our choices, both on a personal and a global scale. In this respect, they are fundamental, more so than any material changes.

Including things that I already mentioned, what are the changes that can be both soft and fundamental? What has to change for us to call it a fundamental change?

I have thought about this a lot. Here is what I propose. We need:

1. A new common identity that is perfectly natural and applicable to all people on the Earth.
2. A new common language that people can use to communicate with each other, without having to learn anything new.
3. A new common goal of life that people can pursue and achieve without having to compete with each other and create winners and losers.
4. A new common scale that fairly values the choices we

make in terms of the benefit to all.

5. A new common activity that everybody can engage in regardless of their conditions, personalities, and backgrounds—and from which they can derive both immediate and lasting benefits.

1. A New Common Identity

The world today is riven by conflict and division. Large groups of people identifying with a particular set of beliefs or with the imaginary borderlines separating Earth into nation-states are endlessly vying for power and control. For a new civilization to be a harmonious civilization instead of a collection of many conflicting factions, we need a new shared identity. The new identity that I propose is Earth citizen.

I see your smile. You may think it sounds like sci-fi, but to me, it is the only true identity that makes sense. All other identities, imposed and limited by cultural, political, and/or religious divisions, don't have anything to do with what we really are.

Because there are billions of galaxies, each containing billions of stars like the sun in our solar system, it is reasonable to suspect that there might be other planets like the Earth where sentient beings like us exist. Suppose that you joined a space expedition and your spaceship landed on one of those planets. Thankfully, the beings on that planet were not hostile, and they welcomed you. Either they or you figured out how to communicate with each other. One of the very first questions they would ask you is, "Where are you from?" What would you say in response? Would you say you are from Arizona or New Jersey? Or from the United States, China, Japan, or Korea? The only answer that makes sense would be that you are from Earth. And this answer will work wherever you go in this universe. It is your universal identity.

We won't need to create a new ID card based on this idea in the near future. However, what we do need is the *sense* of this identity, the thought and feeling that "I am an Earth citizen," before I am American, German, Chinese or Indian; I am an Earth citizen before I am Muslim, Buddhist, Jewish, or Christian. Originally, there were no nations or religions; there was only the Earth. Deep down, this is still true. Becoming an Earth citizen means that you are breaking out of a self-imposed idea of who you are and embracing the broader reality of who you truly are.

Our way of life shows that we are already Earth citizens. Our communications and business transactions all give proof to our lives as planetary citizens. Look at the things you use every day. How many of them are from your local community? If we look into the details, the picture becomes all the more diverse. Even a single electronic device contains components manufactured in many countries all over the world.

Digital communication is the same: one video uploaded at one corner of the Earth can be watched by billions of people all over the world, as was seen with "Gangnam Style" by Korean singer Psy, which became the biggest YouTube hit of all time as of 2013. Most of us regularly talk, email, or videoconference with people all around the globe. The traditional boundaries are being quickly left behind by the current reality of the world. "Earth citizen" is no longer a concept or notion—it is already our reality.

So, what does becoming an Earth citizen mean? Just as the

love of a country does not merely mean the love of the geographical territory, the love of Earth does not only mean environmental concern and activism. Loving Earth also means that above other, more localized allegiances, you recognize yourself as a member of the Earth community. Just as a father will care for his family and a citizen will show loyalty to her country, so will Earth citizens do their best to fulfill their responsibilities and roles in the Earth community, deriving happiness and pleasure from performing such roles and responsibilities.

When we all accept and embrace an Earth-based value system, all the conflicts that came from disagreements among the smaller value systems of the world will seem increasingly irrelevant and will finally disappear. When we all become true Earth citizens, religious differences will be a matter of individual tastes, and ideological disagreements will produce interesting conversations and debates, not wars, persecution, and terrorist attacks. In an Earth community, these differences will no longer cause conflicts but merely represent cultural diversity and richness.

2. A New Common Language

Using language effectively is a challenge. It is also a personal challenge to me. Whenever I talk to an audience anywhere other than in Korea, I wish I could speak their language. Because, although I have an able translator as an assistant, there's always a sense that something is missing, especially when I tell a joke. It's very difficult to translate jokes. We can translate the meaning of the words, but in many cases the nuance that makes a joke a joke is lost in translation. When this happens, I sometimes have to explain, but you know that an explained joke is not a joke anymore.

Language is especially a headache in diplomatic communication. I know this because I have some experience of international conferences with leaders who represented various countries or religions. Some people in these organizations told me that it sometimes takes years to change a single sentence in a document in a way acceptable to all parties involved.

The language we need in order to build the foundation of a new civilization doesn't need to be refined, technical, or sophisticated. Suppose you somehow landed on an island that you didn't know and ran into people there who didn't understand your language. To prevent them from being hostile to you and to enlist their support, you would need to communicate. What would you do? Smiling would be a good place to start. It's a universal expression of friendliness. What else? You may open your arms to show that you don't have anything to harm them. Relaxing your shoulders and lowering your body would also help because a stiff, straight posture would make you look arrogant and threatening.

The language that I propose for communication among all Earth citizens, as a foundation for a new civilization, is even simpler than these gestures. That language is nothing other than LifeParticles. Use LifeParticles at any time, anywhere. Send positive energy to people around you, and to those in any location who need support. In your prayer and meditation, send LifeParticles to people whose lives are more painful and unhappy than yours. You don't need to understand their culture or language. We are all connected in the unity of Energy-Consciousness. LifeParticles can go to anybody at any time and any place.

You will find how powerful this communication is if you use it to help and heal others. When we communicate with others through LifeParticles, we are not doing so in our nationality, culture, or religion. We are connecting as fellow Earth citizens. Or even more fundamentally, we are relating on the level of our true nature as the unity of Energy-Consciousness.

It is the purest and most truthful communication. You can lie with words, but you cannot lie with energy because your energy conveys exactly how you feel, how you are, and what you are. So before you say kind words to others, try to have kind energy for them first. Before you teach your children to say kind words, teach them to have kind energy first.

You may say unkind words with kind energy. It won't hurt other people because they can sense the underlying kindness. However, if you say kind words with unkind energy, it will hurt others more than unkind words with unkind energy, because of the discrepancy between how you are inside and what you profess outside.

Because of the nature of this new language, communication with LifeParticles doesn't need to be limited to taking place between humans. All beings are made of the same nonmaterial material. Send positive energy to other life-forms, or even to inanimate things, and see how they respond. Remember, nothing is as solid as it looks. At the fundamental level, everything exists as waves of probabilities that manifest into physical reality in response to the observation of conscious mind. LifeParticles can be the language for global and universal communication between all Earth citizens, all life-forms, and all beings.

3. A New Common Goal in Life

How would you like to feel at the last moment of your life? Peaceful, satisfied, happy . . . these are the most common responses to this question. Nobody wants to conclude his or her life in regret, shame, or resentment. When all the hustle and bustle of life has settled down and the dust and clouds have cleared away, when you have become able to see things without attachment, the way you feel about yourself and your days on Earth will be all that you have as the grand total of your life. That's why this question, which helps us to see what's really important, is worth asking now.

My answer to this question is "complete." I would like to feel complete at the last moment of my life. Isn't this the way you would like to feel? Happy, satisfied, and peaceful may help, but they don't make you feel complete. You will feel complete only when you are complete.

When you do some action out of kindness, with a genuine intention to benefit others without expectation of any recognition or reward, a feeling of contentment and gratitude arises quietly from inside. I experienced this for the first time when I was in my early twenties. Life was challenging for me then. I had failed the college admission exam three years in a row. In Korean culture at that time, this was a big thing: it meant that I was a *big* loser. I didn't have a dream or any hope for my future. It was hard for me to look at my parents, who expected a lot more from their eldest son.

One day, when I was walking over a bridge, I happened to look down below the bridge, where I saw a pileup of garbage and trash. I felt that the trash was like me—unattended, abandoned, and hopeless, without any use or purpose.

At that moment, a thought came to my mind, that it would be great if I moved the smelly garbage to a field where I could use it as fertilizer to grow pumpkins. Where that thought came from is a mystery—it was completely uncharacteristic of me at the time—but I decided to act on it.

Because it was the middle of summer, and the empty field I decided on was up a fairly steep hill, I became hot and sweaty soon after I started moving the garbage. It took two whole days from dawn to dusk for me to move all of it, even though I was physically fit and strong.

My father became quite angry when he found out what I was doing, and he asked me to stop. He thought I was shaming him. And I have no doubt that some people thought that something was wrong with me. A young person, a known "loser" in a small village, suddenly jumps on a pile of garbage and starts moving it, all in a sweat. . . . I did it anyway, and when I finished, there was a feeling of contentment when I saw the clean area under the bridge and imagined the pumpkins that would be harvested in the fall.

But the greatest feeling of contentment came from the knowledge that I had decided to do something good for the world from my own pure choice, and I had completed it no matter what. There was no thanks or applause, but there was a deep sense of acknowledgement from inside. Soon it turned into a feeling of gratitude. To whom? I didn't know, or it didn't matter at that time. Later I realized that the gratitude was from me to myself, to my true nature, for guiding me to make a right choice. Awakening to the realization that I had within me the desire to do good for others, and the ability to follow through on that noble desire, gave me the motivation to undertake more actions in the same manner. I passed the exam and entered college that year.

When autumn came, as expected there were a lot of big golden pumpkins. I harvested them and gave them away to our neighbors. The neighbors gave me the thanks they had withheld for several months as they waited to see if anything would come of this young man's crazy behavior.

That experience gave me some hint of feeling complete. Even when you become complete, there won't be any *Certificate of Completion* awarded to you. A hardly noticeable gentle smile on your face might be all you have. Other people may not understand why you smile, but that's not what matters to you. That smile is worth a lifetime of sweat and tears, because you have achieved completion.

Until you become complete, there is always a sense of emptiness, a feeling that something is missing in life, like a hole in the soul. Because of this sense of emptiness and meaninglessness, people look around for something to fill the hole: games, food, entertainment, drugs, money, partners, sports, knowledge, power. . . . When we've achieved our goals in these pursuits, we feel good, but the good feelings don't last long because the hole in the soul was not filled: it was just thinly covered. I believe most of the readers of this book know what I am talking about. This hole in the soul, the lack of fullness, is the main drive that keeps us pursuing material things, accomplishment, status, recognition, and also keeps us seeking meaning and facing challenges from our very early moments, when we open our young eyes with wonder to life, until the end. We just don't usually understand what this drive is and how to quiet its thirst until late in the game.

That was how I felt about myself and my life, even into my adulthood. That feeling of emptiness and meaninglessness kept me awake during many nights, and drove me to do things obsessively during the days. Day in and day out, there was no peace. When I finally accepted that this hole couldn't be filled with any material acquisitions or accomplishments, I started to look inside. It was inside me, not outside, that I found the answer to how to fill this hole.

This hole cannot be filled by accumulating objects or by achieving higher levels of "success." In pursuit of external growth in *these* ways, there's always comparison, always greater possibilities for expansion, and you can never reach completion. Imagine the biggest thing that can exist. Did you? OK. Now imagine something just a little bigger than that. It is just like this.

What I'm saying is that there's a serious discrepancy between what we really want and what we usually do to get what we think we want. What we really want is to fill the hole inside and become complete, and what we do is look for success and growth outside. This doesn't mean that seeking outward success is bad or meaningless. It does mean that success will be helpful, meaningful, and satisfying when it is aligned to what you really want in life.

Why don't we pursue *now* the way we desire to feel at the last moment of life, instead of waiting to find, in despair, that we don't feel that way when the moment actually comes? This is what I meant by a new common goal, which is the worthiest and therefore is worth pursuing at any moment in our life. The new common goal that I would propose is "completion," replacing the current goal of "success." This goal can be achieved only when we follow the deepest call of our heart and live by our true nature.

There are many paths through the forests of life, but all paths lead to the same destination as long as we seek completion. Our conscience—the absolute truthfulness, the divine nature—will be our faithful guide on our individual paths. In this quest, there's no comparison or competition. My completion does not prevent others from reaching their completion, and my sense of peace does not lessen others'. We each have to choose this goal and walk this path for ourselves. Nobody can do it for anybody else. We are all companions on this journey to completion. And we can support and inspire each other along the way.

When we have this understanding and awareness, the way we see others and treat others will be different. We may compete on a functional level, but we are all companions on the level of our true nature. There might be a critical moment when you find yourself at a crossroads, with one path leading to completion and one to material success. That's the moment to test your integrity; your conscience will show which way to take.

4. A New Common Scale

As discussed in previous chapters, the new common scale that we can use to evaluate all the choices we make in terms of the benefit to all, is the Earth. Earth is the source of life for all forms of life on our planet. If there were no Earth, then no altars could exist for you to worship your god. Without Earth, no nations would exist, nor political ideologies with which to rule a nation. Because of this basic fact of life, Earth—the good of the Earth, the health of the Earth—is the primary value against which all other values should measured. It is the common ground for all the values we pursue in our lives.

We, humanity, are the most powerful factor in determining the long-term global climate. The ecological footprint that we leave collectively is already one and a half times larger than the planet, and as we have discussed above, this could become as much as five times larger if we don't change our direction. This means that to sustain life we would need to create or borrow four more planet Earths from somewhere. Do you see this happening any time soon?

So it is not the Earth, but *we* who need to change. We have to revise and recalibrate our value systems based on the primary value, the Earth, which is common to all peoples and all life-forms. This is how we'll need to recalibrate our personal scales as well. All our choices and actions should be judged by the effects they have on planet Earth. The Native American tribes who made up the Iroquois Confederacy had a saying, "In every deliberation, we must consider the impact of our decisions on the next seven generations." We need to take a lesson from their wisdom.

When you make choices, please remember: what is good for you but not good for others won't be good for you either, eventually; what's good for you and others but not good for the Earth won't be good for you or others either, eventually; what's good for you, others, and the Earth will be good for all.

5. *A New Common Activity for Life*

What is the one activity that everybody does and has to do regardless of conditions, needs, goals, and backgrounds? It is breathing. This is the single and the only activity that connects all people and all life-forms on this planet, literally. The air I breathe is not separate from the air that you breathe. We cannot divide it any more than we can divide space. The essential fact of breathing is not the movement of the chest or abdomen. What is real in breathing is the air that comes in and goes out through the movements of the chest and abdomen. All life-forms that breathe are actually in the constant flow of the air and more fundamentally, in the constant flow of energy flowing through breathing; and therefore, are inseparably connected in breathing.

As mentioned before, it is the beginning and end of life. Thankfully, this activity is being taken care of automatically by the life system within us, without our having to think about it. Even though it is the most important activity for everyone, because we don't need to think about it, we rarely pay conscious attention to it. However, by giving a little more attention to this activity and by recovering its natural rhythm, there are huge benefits for our physical, mental, and spiritual well-being.

First, as was explained in the previous chapter, breathing, unlike other vital functions such as heartbeat, body temperature, blood pressure, and digestion, is intentionally controllable. At the same time, breathing is the foundation for other vital functions, which means that the other vital functions normally not directly accessible can be regulated indirectly by controlling your breathing. For example we can hardly control our heartbeat or blood pressure intentionally, but we can create changes in their state by controlling our breathing. Breathing is therefore the master key of life.

Second, the way we breathe affects our mind and what it does—thinking and feeling—and you can use this knowledge every day. For example, when you are stressed, if you take three deep breaths before you say or do anything, this will help prevent you from making choices you might regret later. By balancing your breathing, you can control your emotions and calm your mind. From the quiet mind arise the wisdom and insight that help you make good choices.

Third, when your breathing quality is improved, it affects all aspects of your body and mind in a positive way. Changing your whole lifestyle may be a big job. Improving your diet is a challenge. But improving your breathing is something you can do with minimal effort. It just needs your mindfulness. That's all. However, its impact on your overall life and health is far-reaching. If you start in this simple way, expanding the change to other areas of your life will be easier. Basically, if you breathe well, eat well, and sleep well, you will be healthy. If you are concerned about your health, check your breathing first. Feel your breath right now, and start breathing mindfully.

To sum up, these are my suggestions for five foundation stones, all of which are soft and fundamental, for starting to build a new, more joyful, peaceful, balanced, healthier, and sustainable civilization: 1) Earth citizen as a new common identity; 2) LifeParticles as a new common language that people can use to communicate with each other without needing to learn; 3) Completion as a new common goal of life that people can pursue and achieve without having to defeat or even compete with others; 4) Earth as a new common scale with which we can weigh all the choices we make, regardless of our personal conditions or circumstances, in terms of the benefit to all; 5) Breathing as a new common activity that all humanity can practice, enjoy, and benefit from.

You can apply these principles to your life without getting stressed or taking any serious risk. If you are sincere, they will help you create the foundation, from within, for a new mentality and a new perspective, which will lead to new behaviors, new habits, and a new lifestyle. That's a good start. As an increasing number of people adopt these new lifestyles, it will become a culture and grow to be an enlightened society and an enlightened civilization.

A COMMON GOAL FOR A NATION

We can start the transition to a better world by beginning to breathe well and practicing a little bit of meditation. However, to create deep, thorough, and lasting changes, the transformation must extend to organizational, national, and global levels. People breathe but a government doesn't. People meditate but a nation doesn't. We need a goal that we can strive for collectively, which, like completion for individuals, benefits all without having to compete with each other to achieve it.

What can be the goal that applies to all communities on all levels, from a small neighborhood association to a large international institution, regardless of their conditions and needs—a common goal that transcends all cultural, religious, and ideological differences, which all nations and countries can pursue and achieve without threatening other countries and nations?

I propose that this common goal is nothing other than universal welfare: all people living peacefully in health and happiness. To me, welfare means more than just personal well-being, and far, far more than lending a helping hand to people who have fallen on hard times. Let me explain.

When I think of welfare, I envision a social, political, and economic system that enables people to realize their full potential, so that they can be productive and creative, and contribute the maximum to their community and the world as a whole. This can never be achieved only through external institutional structures or technological advancements. Without personal empowerment and awakening, and without recovering conscience and integrity on a personal level, welfare in its most genuine sense is not possible, no matter what governmental or charitable institutions may do or try to do.

I understand how people, particularly in the United States, sometimes feel about "welfare" as it is practiced here, and I want to be perfectly clear that what I am talking about is something different. I believe the programs and practices I have developed over the last decades for personal development and natural health, along with all the concepts, principles, and approaches explained in this book, can serve to establish the foundation of universal welfare at little cost, far lower than the system in place now.

Welfare as I mean it is realistic and measurable, as well as fundamental and global, more so than other more nebulous values such as love and peace. Because there are so many diverse personal, cultural, religious, and political views and taboos about love and peace, I'd guess that the discussion between different groups on these topics might end up with the very opposite result! At least, we can talk with numbers about welfare, which we can't do about love and peace. We will achieve greater results by focusing on an objective foundation first, which can then be used to achieve more subjective values.

The indispensable conditions for true welfare are conscience on a personal level and democracy on a community level. Unless welfare, as a social-political system, is based on conscience, it brings negative side effects such as laziness, inefficiency, unfairness, resentment, and animosity, which are the very opposite of what is intended. Only when the conscience in each of us is awakened and every one of us finds joy and pride in honoring its call can welfare perform its job properly. Everything I have discussed in this book is aimed at building the foundation of conscience as the indispensable condition for all other positive changes that we want to see in our world.

Democracy is a political system that has institutionalized the power of choice. Because of this, it perfectly supports the changes we desire to create. Up to now, we have not been fully utilizing the power of choice incorporated into this system. Utilizing its full power is also a matter of conscience. When people begin to use the power of their awakened conscience, democracy will begin to work at its peak potential, inspiring and facilitating the positive changes not only in our political system, but also in our economical, industrial, and educational systems.

Making changes in systems and institutions sometimes appears complicated and even overwhelming. Even slight changes in the draft of a new regulation, for example, may take months. But what really makes this process complicated is not the process itself or the conditions that the new regulation proposes to address. It is the underlying greed, selfishness, and conflicting interests that are involved. When seen through a filter of greed and selfishness, things look different from how they really are.

Here is a simple example: to a typical, profit-driven corporation, people and nature have no intrinsic worth in themselves, but are merely "resources" to be used to make products that can be sold for profit.

Looking through the eyes of conscience, we can more clearly see what is true and helpful and what is not. We can choose ideologies and behaviors that will work for the welfare of all, and discard what won't. If we make choices using Earth as the central standard, welfare as a common goal, and conscience as the absolute scale, even apparently complex changes may happen more quickly than we imagine.

HOW TO START TO MAKE CHANGES

Because we are so accustomed or attached to things, when we think about changes, we think about things first. For example, if you think about potential changes in your personal life, you will most likely think about your habits, job, relationships, your character or personality, or even the path of your life or destiny. However, these things are already manifested. Things, once manifested, are not easy to change. It is like writing an article. Once you print it out, you cannot change it easily. You may use white paint markers or draw a double line to change something in the article, but the result will look ugly. If you have to change it, you had better do it while it is still a digital file on your computer; meaning, while it is still "soft." Your habits, lifestyle, and the path of your life are "hard" things. The soft ones are your thoughts, words, and actions.

If habits, lifestyles, or personalities are fruits, then thoughts, words, or actions are seeds. Change your seeds and the fruits will change accordingly. This can be shown as a flow like this: *Thoughts* → *Words* → *Actions* → *Habits* → *Character* → *Destiny*.

The first three are soft, and easier to change. What you need is your decision to change and mindfulness to be aware of your thoughts, words, and actions. The three on the right are hard, already manifested, and connected to many other equally hard things. The further you go the left, the softer things become and the easier to change.

As I explained in the beginning of this chapter, this also applies to changes beyond the personal level. We do things too "hard." We should start "soft." The perspective of energy will be very helpful to think in a new, soft way. Instead of trying to change the social structures, systems, and institutions, it will be more effective and less stressful to apply our effort to change the thoughts, words, and actions that run those structures and systems.

Can you think of anything even further left beyond thoughts? Yes, you are correct. It is energy. If you want change in your life, I would say, "Change your energy." That is one of the key messages I wanted to share through this book. Changing our energy is how we become truly genuine and authentic. Here is an example. Between saying kinds words with unkind energy and saying unkind words with unkind energy, which one do you think hurts more? Kind words with unkind energy hurt more because of the hypocritical discrepancy and the lack of integrity. If you want positive changes in your life, please be genuinely positive. Have positive energy.

You may wonder how to maintain positive energy all the time. I would say the optimal energy balance in your body and brain is important. The optimal energy balance inside your body and brain doesn't create positive energy automatically without your conscious choice. However, at least it will help you maintain the positive energy and be less affected by negativity inside and outside.

Let me give you two examples of simple exercises to keep your body and brain in good condition in your everyday life.

Happy Gut Makes Happy Brain

How's your gut today? Does this question sound too crude? But do you know that your gut and your brain are closely related?

The gut has a mind of its own, the enteric nervous system, similar to the brain in your head. This gut-brain actually comes from the same embryonic tissue as the brain-brain. These two brains are still connected via the autonomic nervous system— the sympathetic and parasympathetic nerves—and affect each other very closely. This is the basis for what we commonly call "gut feelings."

When a drug is invented to have psychological effects via the brain, it's likely to have an effect on the gut that the research biochemists didn't think about. A quarter of the people taking Prozac or similar antidepressants have gastrointestinal problems such as nausea, diarrhea, and constipation. Even without taking drugs into consideration, when you are mentally or emotionally stressed, you sometimes experience diarrhea or constipation. Kids diagnosed with autism or ADHD are often found to have irritable bowel syndrome. More optimistically, recent studies have found that improving their intestinal conditions has a positive effect on their brain function. So, to have a happy brain, it's good to have a happy gut.

One exercise that helps to keep your body and brain functioning at their optimal level is an abdominal exercise that directly affects your intestinal health. Simply pull in and push out your abdomen repeatedly. The repetition of this movement strengthens the natural rhythm of your gut and improves its function. The most immediate result is an improvement in digestive and bowel functions. This exercise also helps to improve the other internal organs. Even though we cannot directly touch our internal organs, such as stomach, liver, and heart, we can give them some gentle stimulation by doing this exercise. It is like giving a massage to those organs.

When you do this exercise, use your muscle strength mostly for pulling in, and just let go when you push out. You don't need to synchronize it with your breathing. In the beginning, you may feel some tension in your shoulders and arms. If you do, stop and release the tension by shaking your shoulders and arms lightly before continuing. After repeating about 100 times, please tap around your abdomen lightly and massage your belly gently. You can do this exercise 100 times as a set anytime during a day, totaling 300 to 1,000 times a day according to your condition. This will help activate your gut functions, remove toxic waste, strengthen your immune system, and eventually enliven your brain.

Energy Balance for Optimal Functioning of Your Body and Brain

As you know from experience, your brain functions well when it is cool, and your gut works well when it is warm. Your brain, like the CPU in your computer, is so vulnerable to heat that even an increase of two or three degrees may damage its operation. On the other hand, if your gut is cold, it may cause indigestion, constipation, diarrhea, and an accumulation of toxins. So, a cool head and warm abdomen are the primary indicators of an optimal energy balance inside your body.

When you are stressed, do you know where the tension starts in your body? Very often it starts from your neck, exactly at the point where your neck and skull meet. Raise your hands and put your index fingers in your ears. Imagine a line that connects your two fingers, and another line coming down from the top of your head to your bottom. Where these two lines cross, that's where your neck and skull meet, and where the tension starts when you get stressed. When your neck is stiff, it blocks the natural blood flow and the supply of oxygen to your brain, and your head becomes hot and feels stuffy. This is the reverse of the optimal energy balance of cool head and warm abdomen.

What is the simplest way to release tension from your neck? Yes. Shake it, that is, turn your head from side to side. How can you make your abdomen warm? Give it stimulation.

How? Tap it. Then, if you combine these two, you can quickly and effectively release the tension from your neck and restore optimal energy balance. This is the motion that I developed and named Brain Wave Vibration.

Do you remember Water-up, Fire-down, or cool head and warm abdomen, one of the principles of using LifeParticles explained in chapter three? This is one of the most effective exercises to help create the optimal energy balance of Water-up, Fire-down inside your body. It is a simple yet powerful exercise to keep your brain cool and your abdomen warm. When you are in the state of cool head and warm abdomen, even though you have some stressors, you can handle them easily. With this balance, your body feels comfortable, your heart is peaceful, and your mind is clear and focused.

If a change in our lives requires individually or socially painful sacrifices, it will be difficult to put into effect no matter how necessary that change might be. However, if we start down the road of transformation with simple, enjoyable, and tangible changes, we will soon be prepared to tackle larger issues. This is why I choose to teach breathing, meditation, and natural healing to others. These are what we might call soft human technologies, which help us manage our lives without relying on high-energy, high-tech systems, and experts. These technologies will help to make the transition less stressful, smooth, and even enjoyable.

Let's take a look at our health, for example. By using simple skills and human-scale technology, we can vastly improve our own health, thereby reducing the enormous amount of money (10 percent of annual GDP) spent on health care every year. Through simple exercises—such as gentle body-tapping (lightly tapping your body all over); calisthenics that stimulate the body using stretches, twists, and bounces; and breathing exercises that help you breathe more slowly and deeply—we can make remarkable differences in our physical condition. These types of simple, natural exercise have been used for thousands of years. Such methods cost nothing and of course, do not require surgery or medication. Nor are they psychologically burdensome. They don't even require tools or instruments. All you need is a little practice to make them into habits. If such simple things can save time and energy, and allow you to live a more confident and creative life, and save this society a lot of money to boot, isn't this a great thing?

A CHALLENGE TO CHANGE:
THE NOTION THAT WE NEED TO LEARN

I am going to disclose a big secret to you. People think I am an expert in Energy, Meditation, MindScreen, and LifeParticles. But you know what, I am not much better at these than you are. The difference is that I just do it. You don't need to know everything that you want or need to do from the very beginning. Sometimes having a complete plan and trying to stick to it makes things more difficult. You just need to start, and then keep going.

For example, when I give a lecture, what I usually prepare are just a few key ideas to focus on. Other than that, I just leave everything to the flow. Once I start, I feel relaxed and delightfully energized to interact playfully with the audience. What needs to be communicated comes out naturally through words, gestures, movements, or songs. And even if things don't turn out as expected, why should it be such a big deal? The sky doesn't fall.

I hope you find my sharing helpful because, in many cases, when we think we need to make some changes in our lives, what holds us back from making choices and taking action is the thought that we don't know enough and need to learn more. I have a different view.

Modern life asks of us many hours of "learning." We have to learn how to use the computer, ride the subway, use the ATM machine—and even how to sing and dance. We can't even sing or dance without having someone teach us how! However, the things that maintain life itself are never forgotten. This is because we have never learned them in the first place. Have you ever taken a time out and observed your body breathing by itself, without any conscious effort on your part? Can you feel the incredible mystery and beauty of a simple breath? Think for a moment . . . think about life itself. To whom does this life belong? Who allows us the simple beauty of the breath?

In my lectures, I often play music. The instruments I like to use are either a simple drum or a wooden flute. There is no set melody or rhythm, no set notes or songs. I just play to the natural rhythm of my inner being, which, after a while, coalesces into music, a song, and even a dance. Since I never learned how to play these instruments, I never realized nor cared whether I played them correctly or not. The same goes for my audience. Since they have no idea whether I am playing correctly or not, they enjoy listening to the music and rhythm that I enjoy creating. We all get to enjoy the spontaneous joy of creation.

We are too used to learning and being taught. We feel nervous, or sometimes even guilty, when we don't do things exactly the way we were taught, the way we think we "should." It is such overreliance on the need to learn that is making our society into a world of experts—more and more selective, divisive, and complicated by the minute.

When you had to make an important choice in your life, what made you pause and feel afraid? More often than not, it was probably the idea that you didn't know enough. However, just as we don't need to learn to manipulate the most crucial biological functions in order to maintain life, we don't need to be filled with expert knowledge in order to make the most important decisions in our lives.

Learning does not necessarily make it easier to make these choices. Sometimes an abundance of information and divergent "expert" opinions can complicate and confuse rather than clarify our options. Do we really need that much knowledge to live right? Learning and gathering information can be an excuse for putting off a decision and acting on your choice. No matter how much relevant information you have acquired or how much knowledge you have attained, you will always feel a conflict and a modicum of self-doubt at the moment of choice. Ultimately, it isn't your knowledge that makes the choice: it is your values and your will to be faithful to your values.

THE CHANGES WE WANT TO SEE IN THE WORLD

What are the changes you want to see in the world?

I have some ideas: a shift from nonsustainable to sustainable; from material worshipping to material utilizing; from success pursuing to completion seeking; from self-destructive civilization to self-nurturing civilization; from powers of destruction to powers of healing; from a world of Americans, Israelis, French, Chinese . . . to a world of the children of Earth; from a world of Christians, Buddhists, and Muslims to a world of inner spirituality.

From from a parasitic civilization that cannot even safely dispose of its own garbage to a mature civilization that will pick up what it has dropped, replant where it has harvested, and rejuvenate what it has ravaged.

From a world where people see differences in nations and races to a world where people see the one divine nature in all humans and all sentient beings.

From a world where people become so dependent on experts and authorities that they cannot decide even what to eat and how much to sleep, to a world where all people spontaneously follow the awakened inner light to the fulfillment of their lives.

From a world where people live in inner isolation and non-communication amidst a sea of information, to a world where all of the Earth will communicate with each other without having to learn each other's language.

From a civilization lorded over by a small group of political, religious, and financial elites who use violence and coercion as common tools, to a world where enlightenment becomes common sense and guides the paths of life of all to the common destination; that is, completion.

How does this sound to you? Does it sound too ambitious? Will it be too overwhelming? For many people, this would sound like an impossible dream. However, all great achievements in human history that expanded the possibilities of humanity started from dreaming, from boldly thinking about new possibilities, and from believing in the possibilities with a faith close to foolishness. In two young brothers testing their flying machine; or in a gentleman flying a kite into a stormy sky, intentionally to be hit by lightening—we see a burning passion with a dream. When we stop dreaming and believing in our dream, we stop being human.

What we have to do is not a matter of reinventing the wheel but of turning the steering handle; it all depends upon our choice. What's important is to start, maintain the direction, and be persistent. We already have enough power, technology, and resources to provide clean water, food, and shelter to all people on this planet. We just need to readjust the way we use what we already have. We don't need a genius or a new breakthrough technology for this readjustment. What we do need are the clear goal of global welfare and the genuine intention to benefit all. When we have a clear compelling goal, and the genuine intention to achieve the goal, lots of creative fusions and voluntary collaborations will occur—and will create results far greater than any one of us could achieve, imagine, or predict.

THE POWER OF CHOICE OF
100 MILLION AWAKENED BRAINS

We all know that we have power of choice, but there is a special occasion when this power can have a huge impact on the future of a country—elections. In elections, more than any other time, the power of choice is recognized, appreciated, and feared. Interestingly, there are more than 100 countries that have presidential and/or general elections in 2012 and 2013. This means it is a time ripe for global change. So it's a time when the power of conscience is needed more than ever.

Election is not the only occasion when we can change the direction of a society by the power of choice. The opportunities are much closer than you think. How many times a day do you buy things? When you make a purchase, do you have the awareness that you are actually voting by what you buy? Yes, you are. There's no company that is so strong that it can ignore the choice of consumers. Companies can use their power to try to win the favor of consumers, but they can never ignore the choice of consumers. Depending on your "votes," the company that you voted for or against will promote, modify, or remove their products, thrive or decline.

If we are aware, if we use the power of choice consciously and conscientiously, we can have an enormous impact on the direction of our societies and our civilization.

If only 1 percent of the Earth's population choose to live by the standards of Earth citizens, then Earth's destiny will change. Considering that most studies indicate that Earth's population will reach 10 billion in the near future, 1 percent will be 100 million. The power of choice exerted by 100 million Earth citizens—100 million awakened hearts and brains that make choices by the scale of Earth under the guidance of their conscience and for the benefit of all—will change the world. This is the time to make the choice. You have to make the choice, for no one else will. The start of a new civilization begins with you.

OPENING A NEW CHAPTER IN THE HISTORY OF HUMANITY

Hope is still with us. Let's listen to the call from our heart, and follow the guiding light from the center of our brain. Let's gather our passion and wisdom to realize the true welfare in which all people can live in health and happiness.

Let's gather together, and start talking about this dream and share how excited we are about it. Let's start with feeling our breath, and by breathing more deeply and slowly. In the comfortable breathing that flows without our having to do anything, let's recover our trust in the absolute benevolence of life and let go of our fear. In the energy that flows in and out through our breathing, let's see what we really are and awaken the power of conscience, our divine nature. By following the guide of conscience, let's begin to use the full power of choice in every choice we make, from selecting a leader of a nation to buying a loaf of bread at a grocery store. Let's start this movement, this change from "me" to "we," from the eye of Ego to the eye of Tao, beginning now.

We don't know what the end result will look like yet. Even though we cannot see it, we can feel it through the vibration of greatness that comes from the deepest place in our heart. This vibration tell us that the world we will recreate will be more beautiful than all the beautiful dreams that we dreamed put together, and greater than all greatness we imagined combined. Let's open the first page with this excited, fluttering, hopeful heart. We may stagger for a few steps as we all did when, as toddlers, we first had to learn to stand up and walk. But soon, we will run and take off.

A VERY PERSONAL INVITATION

Please accept this as an invitation to participate in an experiment. If you are interested in creating changes for all, please: share the ideas presented in this book with others, start doing these simple exercises, and send LifeParticles to all who need help and healing. Apply the principles of LifeParticles and test them. If they work for you, share them with others. Many people have already started the movement in their workplaces, communities, schools, churches, and social gatherings.

As we keep creating positive changes in our lives, our experiment will grow, maybe up to the point of creating a new civilization for the greater future of humanity. We don't know exactly what a new civilization will look like. I'd like to call it a spiritual civilization, in the sense that it will be built on more than the material expansion that characterizes the current civilization.

Many people feel that the change has already been initiated. You have been personally invited to this great experiment.

I propose to start this movement by changing our energy.

Change your energy! Be genuinely positive. Have kind energy before you say kind words or do kind gestures. Affect other people positively.

For all who join this movement for change, I propose three simple actions to get started:

1. Take Three Deep Breaths

Take three deep breaths, at least three times a day. By taking three breaths, refresh your mind and energy. If you are stressed, take three deep breaths before you do or say anything. Use the space you get from breathing to make a better choice that can benefit all.

2. Do an Act of Kindness

Out of pure kindness, do something for the world, at least three times a day. Say a warm and caring hello to a neighbor. Remove a rock from a walking or bicycling path. Anything that will benefit the world, even in the smallest way. Note: Bigger ways are okay, too!

3. Send LifeParticles to Other People

Send LifeParticles to at least three people or groups who need the positive energy, without expectation of any recognition or reward. This will benefit not only others but also yourself, because the positive energy will affect you first.

Let's dream about greatness, be passionate about the dream,

and do something every moment for the dream. Together, let's grow in enlightenment and create an enlightened world.

EPILOGUE

Change Is Possible

So, what changes would you really love to see in your personal life and in the world? What changes do you truly desire? You now know that this question will bring you more questions than answers. And that's a good thing.

You also know that in order to make changes happen, first and foremost, you need to have the desire to create changes. For most of us, just identifying what we want or need to change is not enough. It's a good starting point, but you have to have a strong desire. Knowing alone doesn't make us take action. It is our desires that drive us to act.

One of the great and beautiful capabilities of your brain is the simple eagerness to find answers to questions that you ask. Your brain is perfectly capable of and actually excited about performing things you've never done before, or even things you didn't think you could do. When your brain cannot see the way, it will look for a way; and if your brain still cannot find a way, it will create one.

Please do not ever stop asking—no matter what. Keep bothering your brain with unwavering persistence until you find an answer. Go deeper and deeper until you meet with your absolute self, your intrinsic, unalterable true self—your changeless nature. You cannot see or touch it, but you can *feel* it. If you feel it, you can utilize and live it.

It's a wonderful paradox: only when you have a changeless sense of who you are, can real changes take place. The unchanging level of your being is the source of wisdom and power for all change and growth. It is the ground of your absolute value and everything that is truly worthwhile.

When you find the absolute values, you are important to this world because you know what is important. Those who know what is truly important are helpful to this world, because they won't put their personal concerns before what is important for all.

I believe in the goodness of my fellow human beings. We have a true desire for greatness and genuine good intention to be helpful to others. That's enough. Change is possible.

Seriously.

As a final note, I would like to offer you a poem that I wrote about 20 years ago to honor the beautiful changes you will create.

YOUR BEING

Your face
Forever holding the joyous smile,
Your arms
Majestic as a crane's wings,
Your heart
Fiery as a dragon's breath,
Your legs
Sturdy as a stately oak,
Your neck
Graceful as a fawn's bow.

Your eyes
Pierce the emptiness yonder
To draw a world of visions and dreams
Beautiful.

Your head
Lightens the darkness beyond
Wearing a crown of wisdom
Radiant.

Your body
Dances through the clouds above
Streaking across the sky
Limitless.

Your heart

Beats the roar of a lion
Overflowing with an unstoppable will
Calling.

Your hands
Soothing the hurts of humanity
Hands of a bodhisattva
Healing.

Your feet
More fleeting than the fastest steeds
Never tiring
Always.

With a grand will living deep in your heart,
With your eyes fixed upon the vision,
Confidence and peace dawning on your face,
Power infuses your being.

My dear friends: May this day come soon!

ACKNOWLEDGMENTS

I would like to acknowledge Steve Kim for his unwavering support in organizing the material and shaping this book through all of its stages. I would also like to express my deep gratitude to Jack Forem for his thoughtful and thorough editing that captured the spirit of this book. I am indebted to the ancient teachers of the Korean Tao tradition who allowed me to expand my experiences in the light of the great legacy of this knowledge.

RESOURCES

You can find a wealth of information about the change movement and LifeParticles on www.changeyourenergy.com. This website was designed to share the power and possibilities of LifeParticles and our inherent greatness while bringing together a community of like-minded people.

On this website, you can watch the movie *Change: The LifeParticle Effect* and meet many enthusiastic individuals who try to apply the new way of living discussed in this book.

Conceived by Ilchi Lee, this online hub for integrative lifestyle education provides online classes and courses, workshops and retreats, and private coaching and group training that facilitate positive changes for individuals and groups. This website can work as the primary source of tools, resources, and support for those who desire to create positive changes in their lives, share the idea of change with others, and make a difference in their communities. By helping people bring together their passion and inspiration for change, this website seeks to ignite and support an eventual global transition of our lifestyle and culture.

ABOUT THE AUTHOR

Ilchi Lee is an impassioned visionary, educator, mentor, and innovator; he has dedicated his life not only to teaching energy principles, but also to researching and developing methods to nurture the full potential of the human brain.

For over 30 years, his life's mission has been to empower people and to help them harness their own creative power and personal potential. To help individuals achieve that goal, he has developed many successful mind-body training methods, including Dahn Yoga and Brain Education. His principles and methods have inspired many people around the world to live healthier and happier lives.

Lee is a *New York Times* bestselling author who has penned 35 books, including *The Call of Sedona: Journey of the Heart, Healing Society: A Prescription for Global Enlightenment*, and *Brain Wave Vibration: Getting Back into the Rhythm of a Happy, Healthy Life.*

He is also a well-respected humanitarian who has been working with the United Nations and other organizations for global peace. Lee serves as the president of the University of Brain Education and the International Brain Education Association.

For more information about Ilchi Lee and his work, visit www.ilchi.com.

INDEX

absolute scale. *See* common scale; values, absolute and relative

action, defined, 143

analytic vs. contemplative investigation, 36

atoms, 38, 39, 59

attention, defined, 141–42

autonomic nervous system (ANS), 153–54, 197

awareness, defined, 141

balance, energy, brain-body, 197–201; physiological, sense of, 91

being present, in meditation, 149–50; and qualia, 61–62

big understanding, 89, 90, 158

Bohr, Niels, 40

brain, five steps to retraining, 144–48; as key to change, 5; mastering, 148 negative bias of, 21–22; sensitizing, 146

brain-body energy balance, 197–201

Brain Education, 170–71

Brain Refreshing, 147

Brain Versatilizing, 146–47

Brain Wave Vibration, 199–200

breathing, to calm mind, 163–64, 207, 209; as meditation practice, 150–51, 152–57, 158; as new common activity, 179, 190–91, 192; well, for health, 125–26, 129, 130

Buddha, Sakyamuni, 64, 77, 78

calming the mind, 149–52, 158

Capra, Fritjof, 27

cells as independent organisms, 37

change, brain as key to, 5; cost of failure to, 13–17; desire for, and dissatisfaction, 2–3, 6–7; foundation for, 25, 28, 32, 82–83; motivation for, true self as, 185–86, 187, 188, 211–12; movement for, starting,

207–10; as nature of universe, 26–27; social, and conscience, 109–12

change, need for, 12, 13, 175–77; and exponential growth, 14–15, 16–17, 18; and need to slow down, 20–21; and values, 17–19, 109–12 (*see also* recalibration)

Change: The LifeParticle Effect (movie), 6, 217

changes, desirable, summarized, 204–5; how to start making, 195–201; soft and fundamental, 177–92

choice, learning vs. values in, 201–3; power of, 206–7

common activity, new, breathing as, 179, 190–91, 192

common goal, new, in life, 178,184–88, 191–92; for nation, 192–95, 205, 207

common identity, new, as Earth citizen, 178, 179–81, 191

common language, LifeParticles as, 71–76, 80, 178, 181–83, 191

common scale, new, Earth as, 178–79, 188–89, 192; *see also* values, absolute and relative

compassion, 26, 49–50, 51–52, 89

completion as common goal in life, 184–88, 191–92

Connecticut, school shooting in, 12–13

conscience, choosing to acknowledge, 95–98; as condition for universal welfare, 194–95; difficulty of following, 98–102; as experience of Truth, 94–96, 135; and hope, 102–3, 104; power of, 95–98, 102, 103–5,167–69; present in everyone, 95–98; and social change, 109–12

consciousness, nature of, 66–68, 140–41; as source of experience, 63–65;

Superstorm Sandy, 176